Salvation

Scripture

and Sexuality

The Most Rev. Mark Steven Shirilau, PhD
Archbishop of the Ecumenical Catholic Church

With Assistance from:

The Rev. Jeffery Michael Shirilau
Deacon of the Ecumenical Catholic Church

The Rt. Rev. Robert Darrell Hall
Ecumenical Catholic Bishop of Texas

Edition 5.1

Healing Spirit Press

8539 Barnwood Lane ✠ Riverside, CA 92508 ✠ (951) 780-9932
HealingSpirit@ecchurch.org

Copyright ©1992, 1995, 2002, 2011, and 2013 by the Ecumenical Catholic Church.

All rights reserved.

Cataloging Information:

Shirilau, Mark Steven [The Most Reverend Dr.], 1955-
Shirilau, Jeffery Micheal [The Reverend], 1953-1993
Hall, Robert Darrell [The Right Reverend], 1964-
  Salvation, scripture, and sexuality

1. Christianity - salvation in
2. Christianity - social and moral issues in
3. Sexuality and religion
4. Biblical interpretation
5. Homosexuality - religious issues concerning
6. Prostitution – religious issues concerning

ISBN 1-881568-23-7

Printed in the United States of America
Fifth Edition, June 2013. Revision of 1992, 1995, 2002, and 2011 editions

10 9 8 7 6 5 4 3 2 1

Healing Spirit Press
8539 Barnwood Lane
Riverside, CA 92508-7126
(951) 780-9932
Fax (951) 789-0783
HealingSpirit@ecchurch.org

Mark Shirilau is the archbishop of the Ecumenical Catholic Church. He holds master's degrees in religion, business, and engineering and received his doctorate from the University of California at Irvine. Archbishop Mark is an expert theologian, scholar, and professor and is president of an engineering firm specializing in solar power and energy conservation. His background allows him to approach and research the Bible without letting emotion and prejudice get in the way.

Jeffery Shirilau, founding deacon of the Ecumenical Catholic Church and Mark's life-partner, had a background in construction, computer programming, and entertainment. He was a licensed contractor and brought the hands-on, real-world dimension to the team, complementing Mark's academic background.

Rob Hall is the Ecumenical Catholic Church's bishop of Texas. He is a former police chief, emergency medical technician, and pastor of the Austin, Texas, parish, and has served as executive assistant to the primate. He brings a deep contemplative spiritual dimension to the author team.

The Ecumenical Catholic Church is a separate denomination within the universal Christian Church. We share with all Christians the faith of the Nicene Creed – the belief in One Triune God and acceptance of Jesus Christ as the Son of God and Redeemer of humanity. We are united with others through the rebirth of Baptism and the fellowship of the Eucharist. We are committed to clearly presenting God's unconditional love to you and everyone else.

If you wish more information about our church and ministry, and the location of the nearest ECC parish or priest, visit the website at www.ecchurch.org or write to the denomination's headquarters:

8539 Barnwood Lane
Riverside, California 92508

or email Archbishop Mark at Archbishop@ecchurch.org.

Table of Contents

Dedication

This book is dedicated to the memory of Jeffery Micheal Lau Shirilau, founding deacon of the Ecumenical Catholic Church. Jeffery was born on earth August 30, 1953, in Honolulu; born in Christ (baptized) December 9, 1956, in Los Angeles; and born in heaven August 9, 1993, having died in Monte Rio, California. He was buried in Kaneohe, Hawaii, on his fortieth birthday. He was a vibrant source of inspiration throughout his struggle with AIDS and left this world of pain eagerly awaiting his true going home.

It was through Jeffery's persistence in 1991 that this book was first drafted. It was also his direction which led me to prepare a work that went beyond the usual attack on the antigay rhetoric, but also clearly portrayed the Gospel of Jesus Christ -- that salvation is not really a moral issue (sexual or otherwise) at all, but is a free, uninhibited, and unearned gift of God.

Archbishop Mark Shirilau, 1995

Forward

It is truly an honor to be a part of this publication. Having been involved with the Christian and gay communities for over twenty years, I felt a strong need to merge the two groups. This can only come about through education and love. We must all be taught the truth, uncluttered by emotional influences. Many publications and books have been written concerning the "clobber passages" and to a far greater extent than can be found here. The beauty of Bishop Mark's work is that it is centered on what is important to us all as Christians, and that is Salvation and God's unconditional Love for all.

Deacon Jeffery Shirilau, 1992

Truths for All

✠   Jesus loves you, me, and everyone else.

✠   God's Love is not dependent on what we do,
            who we love, or with whom we have sex.

✠   Salvation is a free gift of God's Grace.

✠   Baptism, Communion, and Love are where we
            best encounter this Grace.

✠   Know that your heavenly Father made you
            good as you are,

        That Jesus rose again to give you life
           eternal, and that

        The Holy Spirit speaks to you today.

✠   Know and Believe that God is Love.

We pray that you will do that.

Christianity is not about right and wrong.

Right and wrong are not about sex.

Therefore it is doubly erroneous
to associate Christianity
with sexual narrow-mindedness.

Introduction

One of the greatest sins in our world today is the fact that some people, supposedly speaking as Christians, condemn other people because they do not follow various moral codes found in portions of the Sacred Scriptures. The real tragedy of this activity is that those persons who are told they are wrong often reject Scripture, the Church, and God Himself because they know in their hearts that they cannot change the part of themselves that is supposedly evil. Rather than bringing new souls to Jesus, therefore, the hypocritical preachers of hatred and bigotry actually drive souls *away* from the Fold of Christ. I am certain that preachers such as these will be sorry, embarrassed, and sorely disappointed when they meet their Maker in heaven and He points out the hideous result of their error.

Today the people most sorely persecuted in the name of Scripture are the homosexuals. Persons of this minority group make up an estimated minimum of 10% of the population.[1] One could reasonably conclude that there are at least 700,000,000 gay people alive today in the world.

Whether homosexuality is a result of nurture or nature is a long debate. Gay people argue consistently that they never chose to be homosexual. (This should never be confused with choosing to act upon one's intrinsic homosexuality.) Those people who try to argue that

---

[1] In 1993 there was considerable publicity regarding some studies that reported much lower incidences of homosexuality. These studies, however, were conducted primarily through in-person interviews. Such a research methodology could hardly be considered accurate given not only their lack of anonymity, but also the intimidation of discussing socially stigmatized behaviors with another living person. While this survey method clearly would have counted the bold gay pride activist, it clearly would not have counted the secretive heterosexually married gay man being interviewed in the home he shares with his wife. One could, in fact, argue that even the more typical 10% figure is very low because even it would not accurately reflect the true behavior of those homosexuals who are so deep in denial that they do not even admit their gay sexual activities or desires to themselves. This behavior of "closeted" activity and deep self-denial (let alone admission to even a truly anonymous survey) is far more prevalent than many heterosexuals either suppose or admit. And finally, there is yet another group of homosexuals that the majority of surveys would not detect. Those are the people who are emotively gay or bisexual but have never actually acted upon those emotions. There are a number of causes of such behavior, not the least of which are indoctrination with the prevailing error that homosexuality is among the worst of sins and the ever-present inundation with pro-heterosexual messages that all people in Western cultures receive since birth. Given all the various and powerful factors which keep research numbers (including Alfred Kinsey's) lower than the truth, one cannot help but wonder if there is validity to the philosophical hypothesis that, given a total absence of social stigmatization and pressure, the human populations would be 25% homosexual, 50% bisexual, and 25% heterosexual or, perhaps more accurately, 100% bisexual with a continuum of bisexual inward desire and outward expression.

homosexuality itself is chosen – as if a person chooses whether s/he feels erotically about men, women, or both – are simply not paying attention to reality. Heterosexuals making such ridiculous claims should realize that *they* never woke up one morning and chose to be attracted to the opposite sex, though they may well have awakened one morning and realized that they were heterosexuals.

People are gay, straight, or bisexual as surely as they are white or black, mathematically inclined, artistically talented, black-haired or blond. It is simply part of who someone is. Note, too, that for things such as academic and artistic abilities, no one is entirely sure how much is a result of "nature" and how much is "nurture," yet we accept that some people are artistically or mathematically inclined, while others are not.

Furthermore, the nature/nurture debate is essentially irrelevant from the standpoint of civil rights. Race is clearly a matter of "nature" in this debate, and religion is clearly a matter of "nurture," yet each is equally protected by civil rights. Furthermore, civil rights in a modern political system are always disconnected from the moral codes of religions since, at least in the Judeo-Christian-Muslim tradition, obedience to the One True God, and Him alone, is the highest moral duty.[2] While the merits of the American repudiation of the First Commandment can be argued, one cannot argue that American freedom of religion is consistent with the Ten Commandments.

Furthermore, one cannot argue within the modern political system that freedoms and rights should be attributable only to aspects of nature, and not to socially nurtured concepts such as religion and political affiliation. Therefore, the nature/nurture debate about homosexuality, while interesting at both a biological and psychological level, is irrelevant when it comes to protecting gays, lesbians, bisexuals, transgendered persons, and other sexual minorities with equal rights under the law.

Yet gay people, in spite of the fact that they surely populate the highest ranks of government, academia, the business world, and the Church, still have to fight hard to be guaranteed even the most basic rights. Incidents of birth like race, gender, and nationality are protected against discrimination by most governments. Nondiscrimination laws even protect

---

[2] The First Commandment – also the one that Jesus said was the most important – is "I Am YAHWEH, your God, you shall have no other gods before Me." The American concept of "freedom of religion," therefore, is based in its very roots in the discarding of the Ten Commandments, or at least the most important one of the ten.

incidents of choice such as religion. It is both strange and sad, therefore, that sexual orientation is usually not protected. It is even more tragic that some outspoken, well-meaning, but terribly misguided Christians are often at the forefront of this bigotry.

Worse yet, millions of gay people are left feeling inferior, unwanted, and even unloved by God. This is a needless tragedy that can be overcome by the Truth. This book hopes to be a beacon of that Truth within a world clouded by the lies of evil. "God hates" is the most basic and most evil of all lies, and yet it is heard day after day from persons termed "religious leaders" in our culture. Surely Jesus sheds a tear of sorrow every time He hears this lie. Many, many innocent people succumb to suicide, drugs, despair, and abandonment needlessly because they have been lied to in God's Name. Anyone who would suggest that God hates part of what He created would do well to pray and meditate on the Second Commandment, so very well translated in the New Revised Standard Version of the Bible: "You shall not make wrongful use of the Name of the LORD your God, for the LORD will not acquit anyone who misuses His Name." (Ex 20:7)

It is our fervent prayer that the truths portrayed in this book will enlighten the paths of many such persons caught in despair because they have been lied to – by family, friends, pastors, politicians, and others normally worthy of respect. Furthermore, it is also our hope that those who are now preaching the message of hatred will turn around and learn the wonderful Gospel of Love that our Lord came to proclaim to each and every person.

In 2011 the book was expanded to include a discussion on the concept of "*Sancta Mater Ecclesia*" or "Holy Mother Church" and its impact on people's understanding of morality and self-acceptance. Having been raised in Anglican-Protestant traditions, we authors focused almost entirely on Scripture and reason, which have basically intellectual effects on the worldviews and moral compasses of individuals. After years of ministry with persons raised with Roman Catholic backgrounds, particularly in regions where Roman Catholic culture dominates, we became aware of the great impact that the concept of "Holy Mother Church" plays on these people. This is primarily an emotional impact juxtaposed to the intellectual impact of scriptural interpretation.

In 2013 a comprehensive chapter dealing with "prostitution" was added in order to address the erroneous translations and interpretations surrounding that concept. This awareness first became apparent as the Ecumenical Catholic Church began directed social ministry to help sex workers in a non-condemning manner. We soon realized two obvious yet elusive facts. The biblical passages translated to imply discussion of modern "prostitution" are just as erroneous as those translations implying discussion of modern homosexuality. Furthermore, most writings (including this book's previous editions) exposing the bad translations about homosexuality are content to leave the burden of sin on prostitutes. This is both inaccurate and shameful.

No one would argue that being a prostitute is a matter of either nature or nurture (though for some it may not truly be a matter of free choice). This, however, is irrelevant to the fact that most of the Bible's discussion of "prostitution" bears little if any correlation with modern commercial prostitution or sex work.

The Bible

It is always important to have a basic understanding of what is being discussed, so a discussion of Scripture ought first simply address what Scripture is and what it is not. Some of the problems that arise when people either use or reject Scripture are associated with two words: *fundamentalism* and *inerrancy*.

"Fundamentalism" is a modern movement within the Church arising in the late 1800s as a counter to the developing knowledge and research in history, science, and the humanities. Part of the growing scope of human understanding shed new light on religion, and some secularists tended to carry this to the extreme, relegating religion to the back burner or even throwing it out altogether. "Fundamentalism" was supposedly a call back to five basic principles: (1) the authority of Scripture, (2) the Deity of Christ, (3) the atonement of Christ on the Cross, (4) the Resurrection and Ascension, and (5) the literal return of Christ.

In fact, fundamentalism shares only the middle three of these "fundamentals" with orthodox Christianity. The Church has always given authority to Scripture, and the Nicene Creed clearly professes, "He [Christ] will come again to judge the living and the dead." However, the fundamentalists placed an emphasis on these minor doctrines – Scripture and the Second Coming – that had never before been made. Fundamentalists made the Bible literally inerrant for the first time.[3] The fundamentalists also concentrated on the idea of Jesus coming in the near future to somehow complete what He had not yet completed; they made this future event as important as His coming in Bethlehem at Christmas. These two concepts of biblical inerrancy and the "rapture" were essentially invented in the late 1800s, yet they were portrayed by some as essential and fundamental articles of faith![4]

---

[3] One must distinguish between belief in ancient myths and belief that the Bible is literally inerrant. It is certainly true that before modern scientific discoveries most people (including the apostles and the reformers) believed the Genesis creation stories were historically factual. However, we must carefully note that this is only because they had no evidence to the contrary, *not* because such literalism was a key issue in their theology. To claim that such historical Christians would take such a literal approach if they were alive today is as ludicrous as claiming that Isaac Newton, if alive now, would rigorously defend his technically out-dated views of physics against the later developments of relativity and quantum mechanics.

[4] See, for example, Dr. Lloyd J. Averill, *Religious Right, Religious Wrong*. New York: Pilgrim Press, 1989.

"Inerrancy" is the concept that the Bible is technically inerrant in every detail. Its contenders hold the absurd concept that "if you cannot believe everything, you cannot believe anything." That is somewhat like saying you would never listen to any of Bach's music because he wrote one piece you did not like. Preachers of inerrancy like to imply that the great Christians of the past, particularly the various reformers, believed in a similar concept. This, of course, is simply not true.

Inerrancy's supporters also contend that the Bible itself supports inerrancy. This, too, is not true. One passage (2 Timothy 3:16) speaks of Scripture as "inspired by God," but "inspired" does not imply "inerrant." Furthermore, it is rather irrelevant what Scripture says about itself. If such circular logic were valid, we would all certainly have to believe in papal infallibility because the pope himself believes in it.

Inerrancy is so illogical that it is curious that anyone could seriously believe in it, yet all of us have probably met people for whom this concept is as vital to their understanding of Christianity as the Resurrection itself. For example, it is funny that the fundamentalists have such a problem with evolution because it is supposedly inconsistent with Scripture, but Genesis is not even consistent with itself. In Genesis 1:26 we read that God made man after He had made all of the other animals. Man (and woman) was to be the crown of creation. In Genesis 2:18-19 we read that man was alone and that God made all of the animals to be his helper. So which came first, the beast or the human being? The Bible presents two different (and logically irreconcilable) answers.

Modern scholarship tells us that two different people wrote these two chapters of Genesis at two different periods in Israel's history. The two stories approach the whole relationship between God and humanity in different ways. Both stories and their authors tell us the most important point – that God created all that is. Otherwise, the two stories address different concepts of our relationship with nature, and neither author was trying to answer scientific questions in the same manner as a modern paleontologist would. Sadly, it was the development of this type of modern biblical scholarship that gave rise to fundamentalism in the first place.

So presumably we have made clear one thing that the Bible is not – some sort of literally inerrant dictation from God transcribed in a mechanical fashion by human stenographers. Some well-meaning (and some not so well-meaning) Christians believe this fallacy even though the idea is both a modern invention and is inconsistent with traditional Christian teaching. Furthermore, the concept of inerrancy is flatly dangerous. It gives rise to hideous perversions of the Truth because the Holy Spirit is rendered essentially powerless and God's Love is made subordinate to the words of a book.

Thomas Troeger spoke well of the importance of both faith and reason, Scripture and science, in a hymn:[5]

> May our faith redeem the blunder
>   of believing that our thought
> has displaced the grounds for wonder
>   which the ancient prophets taught.
> May our learning curb the error
>   which unthinking faith can breed
> lest we justify some terror
>   with an antiquated creed.
>
> As two currents in a river
>   fight each other's undertow
> till converging they deliver
>   one coherent steady flow,
> blend, O God, our faith and learning
>   till they carve a single course,
> till they join as one, returning
>   praise and thanks to You, their Source.

What the Bible truly is, then, is a story of God's love affair with humanity. It tells of a loving Creator Who made all of the universe in order to have real spiritual beings that could love Him back out of their own free will. It tells of how this creating Father struggled with His children to teach them the way of Love, how they did not always grasp what real Love is, and even how they sometimes made God into their own image (such as some of the "warrior-God" passages of the Old Testament).

Finally, the Bible is the story of the Word of God Who entered His very own creation, not as a book or a stone tablet, but as a helpless Baby in a manger. It tells of how Jesus grew and taught and healed, of how He was killed for our sins and rose again in triumph. It tells of

---

[5] "Praise the Source of faith and learning," Hymn 411 in *The New Century Hymnal* (Cleveland, OH: Pilgrim Press, 1995)

how He gave His own Body and Blood to be our Food for eternity. It tells of how the Holy Spirit came to the Church and how He would be God-with-us for evermore.

The Bible is to the Church as the Constitution is to the United States. It is the creation of the Church, since it was the faithful people before and after Christ who wrote it and it is the councils of the Church that decided what writings were and were not "the Bible." On the other hand, it is the foundation of the Church because it is set concretely in history and contains within itself every bit of knowledge that is absolutely essential for being a Christian.

Pharisees, Fundamentalists, and Jesus

The most puzzling thing about modern fundamentalists is that they so fit the patterns of the Pharisees that Jesus spent the most time arguing against. In the Gospels we find story after where Jesus condemns the Pharisees and holds them up against those that the Pharisees condemn. We all know the stories. The Pharisee is always the loser. Jesus eats with the tax collector and the "sinful woman"[6] while he blasts out against the Pharisee. It does not take a long stretch of the imagination to see Jesus sitting at dinner with a gay couple and a porn star criticizing a televangelist.

Because this point seems to be so easily missed by the fundamentalists, in spite of its abundant clarity, it does us well to rehearse it.

Jesus condemns the Pharisees for being more concerned about how others see them than about what they believe in their hearts. They emphasize trivial externalities while they ignore the spirit of the law. We have the story of the Pharisee and the tax collector (Luke 18:9-14), where the tax collector's humility is more appealing to God than the Pharisee's diligence in prayer, fasting, and tithing. Matthew 23 expounds on how the Pharisees look for public display of piety and focus on the insignificant, but easily viewed, aspects of religious life.

It is worth noting that one of the things that is ultimately so appealing about the easily viewed trivia that fundamentalists and Pharisees focus on is that these things are ultimately easier to achieve than a pure loving heart. They are mechanical in nature and thus one knows

---

[6] This woman in Matthew 7 is often assumed to be a "prostitute" even though the Bible merely calls her a "sinner."

when one has achieved them. We all can calculate whether or not we have tithed. It is more difficult to determine whether we have truly loved our neighbors as we have loved ourselves.

The legalism of Jewish Pharisees and Christian fundamentalists makes laws and regulations into idols. Jesus points out that this is putting human laws, rather than God, in our hearts (Mark 7:5-9). There are many parables that point out this problem. Many of them use the Sabbath regulations as the example. Mark's Gospel tells of the disciples picking grain on the Sabbath (2:23-28) and compares it to King David and his army eating the sacred Temple grains when they were needed. Perhaps a more clear story demonstrating the dysfunction of rigid adherence to moral regulations is the story in Mark 3:1-7 where Jesus healed a person on the Sabbath. The Pharisees were deeply offended by this, and Jesus was even more offended that they would even think twice before doing what was good and right, just because it had the appearance of immorality.

Today we do not use Sabbath observance as a focal point of morality, but such was not the case in Jesus' day. The Pharisees were as obsessive about the Sabbath and the moral laws around it as modern fundamentalists are obsessive about sex and the moral laws around it. There is a direct parallel. Just as rigid Sabbath regulations kept the Pharisees from really understanding God's Love two thousand years ago, so rigid sexual regulations keep fundamentalists from really understanding God's Love today.

Jesus calls the moralism of His day a heavy burden and accuses the Pharisees of placing these yokes upon others. (Matthew 23:4). We are all familiar with Jesus' statement about burdens: "Come to me, all you that are weary and are carrying heavy burdens, and I will give you rest. Take My yoke upon you, and learn from Me; for I am gentle and humble in heart, and you will find rest for your souls. For My yoke is easy, and my burden is light." (Matthew 11:28-30, *NRSV*).

And St. Paul reminds us of this again, "For freedom Christ has set us free. Stand firm, therefore, and do not submit again to a yoke of slavery." (Galatians 5:1, *NRSV*).

Most compelling of all, Jesus points out the ultimate contradiction between this attitude and the very basis of evangelicalism – the Great Commission to bring others into the Kingdom of heaven. "But woe to you, scribes and Pharisees, hypocrites! ***For you lock***

people out of the Kingdom of heaven. For you do not go in yourselves, and when others are going in, you stop them." (Matthew 23:13-14, *NRSV*).

What more can we say? Moralism stands condemned by our Lord Himself, contradicting the very purpose of the Gospel.

Sexuality and Faith

Our society is hung up on sex. By this I do not mean that every soap opera rotates around various sexual affairs, but rather that we have a destructive paranoia of dealing naturally with the sexual functions that are so very much a part of our nature. Unfortunately, this paranoia is not new, but deeply permeates our Western culture. Because the obsession is so pervasive, it has entered subtly into our religious thoughts, into places where sexuality actually has no place at all. In fact, most people confuse cultural concepts about sex and marriage with religious concepts.

A good example is the present-day assumption that monogamy is the only acceptable lifestyle for a Christian. It is certainly bizarre that a fundamentalist would believe so. After all, many of the heroes of the Old Testament were polygamous. The twelve sons of Israel were in fact four sets of half-brothers, born of Jacob's two wives and two concubines. Kings David and Solomon had several wives, and this was not viewed as evil or even listed among their many moral imperfections. Culture, not religion, has decided that monogamy is best.

There may be justice and fairness issues that raise questions about the moral rectitude of certain aspects of polygamy. Such, of course, can be said of many monogamous relationships as well. In any case, Muslims share the same religious tradition as Christians and Jews and yet they do not see anything specifically wrong with polygamy *per se*.

Likewise, "fornication" is a much-misunderstood concept in the Bible. The Greek word πορνεια (*porneia*) occurs many times in Scripture along with various related words.[7] Through the course of linguistic evolution, many Greek words beginning with "P" moved into English as words beginning with "F" (such as *pater* becoming "father.") *Porneia* in English, therefore, became "fornication."

But in so transliterating (as opposed to translating) the word, we have been grossly unfaithful. For whatever reasons, "fornication" has come to mean any sex outside of marriage, particularly premarital sex. *Porneia*, however, meant "prostitution."

---

[7] Including πορνος (*pornos*), a male "prostitute" and πορνα (*porna*), a female "prostitute," although these were not prostitutes in the modern sense.

To make the story even worse (and to make *porneia* even less relevant to us), this prostitution was radically different from what we think about today. It did not refer to women in gold miniskirts (or men in torn jeans) freely choosing to walk up and down the streets offering sex in exchange for money. Sometimes it referred to slaves brought by "pimps" to a new city and forced to have sex for the financial gain of their owners. Often it meant priests and priestesses of the pagan gods who had sex with the faithful as part of the fertility cult. The idea was that if you wanted a good harvest, you would go to the temple, make a monetary offering, and have sex with the priest or "temple prostitute." Since sex was associated with fertility (appropriately so), this act would please the gods and cause them to send a fruitful harvest.

In fact, the Hebrew words used for these prostitute-priest(esse)s were קָדֵשׁ *(qadesh)* and קְדֵשָׁה *(qedeshah)*, which technically meant "holy man" and "holy woman." In the Septuagint (the ancient Greek translation of the Old Testament) these words were sometimes translated as *pornos* and *porna*.

The problem with *porneia*, then, was not that it was such a bad thing sexually, but that it was idolatry! This also gives us insight as to why the concepts of adultery (which basically means "making impure") and idolatry are so intimately connected in the Bible. In fact, adultery is often used not as immorality in itself, but as a symbol for the greater evil of idolatry.

The Bible simply does not address the concept of premarital sex as we know it. How sad, then, that not only the fundamentalists, but most Christians and even nonreligious people, would swear that it does. Even most Christians who readily practice premarital sex probably believe that the Bible says it is wrong and thereby carry with them some sort of latent guilt. All this is caused by misinterpretation and taking words from one cultural setting and putting them into another.

Our basic point is that sexuality has *nothing* to do with salvation. Sexuality is part of our nature; it is no more or less sacred than breathing. It is no more or less profane than breathing. A person is *not* saved because he or she lives a chaste life. A person is not a saint because he or she dies a virgin. A person is not damned by being gay or working as a prostitute or having an extramarital affair. There may be sexual activities and lifestyles which are degrading, disrespectful of one's partner, unloving, and otherwise immoral, but they are not what hell is all about, and staying away from them is not what heaven is about. Heaven has to do with our relationship with Jesus, not our sexuality.

Salvation

The fair question that follows, then, is "What is salvation?" The idea of "being good" is so intertwined with "going to heaven" in our minds that it is often difficult to wipe this non-Christian notion from our thoughts. I will not go to heaven because I do good. Christianity is not a moral system; it is God's offering of free grace to us.

Jesus says it very clearly in John 6:51:

> "I AM the Living Bread which has come down from heaven.
> Anyone who eats this Bread will live forever;
> and the Bread that I shall give is My Flesh, for the Life of the world."

The Incarnation and the Passion are wrapped up in the Eucharist. The Word of God, the Creating Love that made the world, became a Human Being. He lived among us as Jesus of Nazareth. At the Last Supper He gave us His Body and Blood through the Eucharist, the Sacrament of Holy Communion. This is the new miracle of Incarnation – that bread and wine become the Body and Blood of Christ – and furthermore, when we as baptized children of God eat of this Sacred Food, *we too* become the Body of Christ. "Those who believe and are baptized will be saved" (Mark 16:16). Our belief is made real at the altar when we receive our incarnate Lord.

Pay close attention to that word *anyone*. "Anyone who eats this Bread will live forever." When you hear it, understand that this saying comes straight from the Heart of God. If there is any part of the Bible that literally and inerrantly is the Word of God, it has to be the "I AM" statements of Jesus.

In the Old Testament God revealed His Name as "I AM" (EHYEH in Hebrew), which becomes YAHWEH (He Who Always Is) in the third person. This word is often translated as LORD (with capital letters) because the Jews considered it too sacred to pronounce and substituted the Hebrew word for "Lord" (*Adonai*) in its place. The Septuagint picked up this tradition and translated YAHWEH as Κυριος (*Kyrios*), the Greek word for "Lord."

The traditions of the time called for scholars to quote earlier scholars, much as many academicians do today. One rabbi would say, "As Rabbi So-and-So taught, …" Or else they would quote the Scriptures. The prophets themselves quoted God, often with words such as "YAHWEH says ..." When Jesus simply said, "I AM ...," He not only was speaking with self-authority, but He was appropriating the Sacred Name of God. It is for this supposed blasphemy that the Jews tried to stone Him right after His "I Am the Good Shepherd" discourse (John 10:7-33).

So we have Jesus, the Word of God made Flesh, speaking in direct address by His own authority saying "Anyone who eats this Bread will live forever." *This is the message of salvation.* This is <u>the</u> central Truth of all of Scripture.

This is how we can be *certain* of Life Eternal, not because we are chaste or pure or heterosexual or monogamous, but because Jesus pours out His Blood and *makes us His Body*. God chooses to incarnate Himself in *our own flesh*, imperfect though it be! As Easter Day tells us, *that flesh can never die*.

Homosexuality and Scripture

Hopefully we have very clearly pointed out that salvation is absolutely *not* dependent upon anything sexual and that nothing sexual is a roadblock to salvation (for "anyone" certainly includes persons with all kinds of sexual quirks, even including promiscuous gays and sex workers). We believe it is still important to address some of the scripture passages that have been used to condemn homosexuality and to put these passages in their proper light.

Fundamentalists continue to be the primary roadblocks to fair and equal treatment of gay people in the social system. In fact, this bigotry among these fundamentalists is not actually triggered by the Bible, but is a bigotry they already have and merely try to use the Bible to support the existing thoughts. A perfect case in point is a personal conversation I once had with a homophobic fundamentalist.

This man's basic point was that he used to be an atheist and then became a Christian and now felt the need to fight against the evils of homosexuality. I asked him what he thought about homosexuality when he was an atheist. He said that he has always thought that homosexuality was disgusting. To this comment I replied, "Then you proved my point, it really has nothing to do with religion, does it?" As is so often the unfortunate case with fundamentalists, he failed to see the point.

Anyway, as long as there are people throwing scripture passages in the air, it is important to discuss them one on one. We will present each verse and discuss scholarship and Christian interpretation that will help gay Christians accept what the Bible does and does not say about their lifestyle.

Adam and Eve (Genesis 2:18-24)

Actually, this story is one of the least used against homosexuality, other than in the form of the derogatory (but somewhat humorous) quip, "God made Adam and Eve, not Adam and Steve."

The passage, of course, does not speak of homosexuality at all. It does imply that heterosexuality is both part of nature and blessed by God. I am sure that most homosexuals would readily agree with both of those premises. Heterosexuality is part of nature, and heterosexual relationships are blessed by God.

To conclude, however, that homosexuality is not part of nature or is not blessed by God is simply not a logical emanation from the story. Homosexuality certainly *is* part of nature. Not only are we learning more and more how deeply ingrained this orientation is in the nature of many human beings, but we are also learning more and more how frequently homosexuality occurs among other species of animals. (There are, for example, the whiptail lizards of the genus *Cnemidophorus* that only exist as females, with each lizard being capable of producing fertile eggs by herself. The normal reproductive patterns of this lizard, however, include sexual activity between two individuals [obviously both females], not for the purpose of fertilization, but simply to stimulate the egg-laying response.) Male homosexual activity has been observed among a wide variety of animal species, including most of our closest simian relatives, and as many as 80% to 90% of male bottle-nosed dolphins are estimated to live in monogamous (though not sexually exclusive) sexually active male-male pairs for their entire adult lives, breeding with females during the mating season.[8]

It is simply erroneous to conclude from the Adam and Eve story that only male-female unions are blessed by God or that it is God's desire that every person enter into a heterosexual marriage. The story does not attempt to address every possible relationship – the polygamy of Abraham, for example. Nor does it address the problems of incest that arise if one takes the story literally and assume that the only women available for Adam and Eve's sons to marry would have been either Eve herself or her daughters.

The story, of course, is not meant to be historical fact. (After all, it radically disagrees with Genesis 1.) It is meant to explain a situation observed in human nature – that other animals are good helpers to humans, but that the truly blessed, loving relationships occur between human beings.

---

[8] *Bological Exuberance: Animal Homosexuality and Natural Diversity* by Dr. Bruce Bagemihl (New York: St. Martin's, 1999) is an excellent compendium of the vast abundance of homosexual activity among mammals and birds. The book tends to be a bit scholarly and detailed, but in its 751 pages, it is made absolutely clear than homosexual activity is well within the realm of nature.

Curiously, in colloquial and even some "scholarly" discourses, the story of Adam and Eve is used to justify the importance of heterosexuality in establishing some sort of supposed balance between the "male" and "female" aspects of nature. But such an interpretation is in fact directly *contradictory* to the very story itself. When we read the story carefully, we see that the thing that delighted Adam about Eve was not that she was different, but that she was *the same as he.* In other words, Adam was excited by Eve's *humanness,* not her femaleness. This is so very obvious when we think about it – and yet we are so used to thinking the other way that we don't even notice our error.

This story reads, "YAHWEH God shaped man (*'adam,* ανθρωπον) from the soil of the ground." [Gen 2:7]. Later it reads,

> "YAHWEH God said, 'It is not right that the man (*'adam,* ανθρωπον) should be alone. I will make him a helper (*`ezer,* βοηθον).[9] So from the soil YAHWEH God fashioned all the wild animals and all the birds of heaven … but no helper (*`ezer,* βοηθον) suitable for the man (*'adam,* Αδαμ)[10] was found for him. Then, YAHWEH God made the man (*'adam,* Αδαμ) fall into a deep sleep. And while he was asleep, He took one of his ribs and closed the flesh (*basar,* σαρκα, "meat") up again forthwith. YAHWEH God fashioned the rib He had taken from the man (*'adam,* Αδαμ) into a woman (*'išah,* γυναικα), and brought her to the man (*'adam,* Αδαμ). And the man (*'adam,* Αδαμ) said: 'This one at last is bone (*`etsem,* οστουν) of my bones, and flesh (*basar,* σαρξ) of my flesh!

We have the human being rejoicing over another human being. How much better that human-human companionship was to be than the companionship provided by the dog or cat, cow or sheep, aardvark or zebra. The man rejoiced in the *similarity* – "bone of my bone, flesh of my flesh" –, not the difference, of his companion. He was not rejoicing in the femininity, as if this were something magical. He had already seen female animals. He hadn't yet seen his own kind!

---

[9] The word *`ezer,* "helper," is used in Exodus 18:4 to describe God, where it is given as the derivation of the name of Moses's son Eliezer, *'Eli-`ezer,* "God, my Helper." The Septuagint also uses βοηθος in the translation of the meaning of the name. Βοηθος derives from βοηθεω, meaning "to help," or "to come to the aid of." *`Ezer* is one of four words in Hebrew that can mean "wife." The others are *išah* ("woman"), *ra'yah* ("lover"), and *zugah* ("partner" or "mate").

[10] Note here that the Septuagint translation has switched from translating the meaning of *'adam* as *anthrōpos* ("human being") to interpreting it as a proper name and <u>transliterating</u> it as Αδαμ, "Adam."

And for those who contend that heterosexual marriage is the main emphasis of the Adam and Eve story, we can explore further still:

> "This is to be called woman (*'išah,* γυνη)[11], for this was taken from man (*'iyš,* ανδρος). This is why a man (*'iyš,* ανθρωπος) leaves his father and mother and becomes attached to his wife (*'išah,* γυναικα, 'woman'), and they become one body (*basar,* σαρξ, 'flesh')." [Gen 2:18-24].

The statement is profound. "This is why a man …" How often that is so sadly misquoted. "This is why a man leaves his parents and joins himself to his wife." Why? Because "*it is not good that the human being should be alone.*" Here we have it, in Genesis, the original purpose of marriage – *companionship*![12]

So far in the story reproduction has not been mentioned. We cannot correctly say that reproduction is "why a man leaves his father and mother." Nor can we say that the reason is some sort of mystical union between male and female, as if the male-with-female component were the magic of the bond. While certainly there is magic in the bonds of many males and females, the real magic is the *love* in the companionship. The magic is related to the

---

[11] The Hebrew word *'išah* means "woman" as distinguished from *'iyš,* "man" in the male sense (as opposed to the generic human sense). The Genesis story actually explains the origin of the Hebrew words *'iyš* and *'išah* as much as it explains men and women themselves. The play on words works in English since the word *woman* contains the word *man* just as *'išah* somewhat contains *'iyš.* But note that it does not work in the Greek (or in many other languages). The Septuagint's Greek words γυνη (*gyne,* "woman," hence "gynecology") and ανδρος (*andros,* "[male] man," hence "androgen") have no direct linguistic relationship with each other. The words γυνη and γυναικα are the same, being merely the nominative (subject) and accusative (object), respectively. Curiously, the Latin Vulgate uses *virago* and *vir. Vir,* related to English *virile,* would be the expected term for "[male] man," as compared with *homo,* the generic term equivalent to ανθρωπος and a cognate of the English word *human.* But *virago* is not the normal term for woman (which is *mulier,* with *femina* also being a common direct counterpart to *vir.*) *Virago* means "female warrior." It does, however, preserve the linguistic play on words in perhaps the most unique way. It is a grammatically feminine derivative of *vir,* which had the connotation of "he-man" (hence "virility") and commonly was used to mean "warrior." Quite literally in the Vulgate, then, Adam's companion was essentially termed "the female virile one." It is not actually clear in Hebrew that *'iyš* and *'išah* are as closely related as the story implies. In ancient Hebrew, written without vowels, *'iyš* appears איש **AYŠ** and *'išah* appears אשה **AŠH** (with **A** represent the silent *aleph*). As such *'išah* is indistinguishable from *išeh,* also **AŠH,** which means "sacrifice."

[12] It is deeply profound that the original purpose of marriage, when viewed from both the Bible and observance of our nearest evolutionary relatives, is the same. God gave Eve to Adam in order to fulfill his need of companionship. Chimpanzees form same-sex pair-bonds (see *Biological Exuberance* referenced above) primarily for enjoyment and companionship (and clearly not for reproduction).

similarity of the two, not their differences, and it has absolutely nothing to do with some supposed "complementarity" of male and female.[13]

In leaving the creation stories, we must remember that they are stories written to explain something that was supposed to have taken place before memory. It was not meant to detail an exact historic sequence, a specific event, or two individual people. That is why the Bible's first editors had no problem putting the first and second stories side by side, even though they do not match one another regarding the historical sequence of the events they describe. Genesis 1 has all of the animals (Gen 1:24-25) made before people (Gen 1:26-27). Genesis 2 has all of the animals (Gen 2:18-190 made after Adam (Gen 2:7) as attempts to find him a suitable `ezer or partner.

There are people who say that the story of God creating Eve for Adam means that marriage should be between one man and one woman: "That this is how God intended it," they claim. That argument fails because the story was not meant to describe what God actually did, but to describe the existing human condition. In the case of Adam and Eve, it was meant to describe why people form close bonds with specific individuals. A heterosexual dyad was used in the example, but that example does not preclude either a homosexual dyad or a polygamous relationship from fulfilling the same basic functions.

Furthermore, we must always be ready to take the Bible for what it says, without reading anything else into it. (This caveat should apply especially strongly to biblical literalists). Genesis 2 clearly says that *companionship* is the purpose of the marital relationship. It also says that the thing that excited Adam about Eve was that she was *like* him, not that she was different from him. It was her humanness, not her femaleness, that facilitated the special companionship.

---

[13] This false "complementarity" issue not only permeates some Christian theology, but also many esoteric or "New Age" concepts and even science fiction. There is no indication that "male" and "female" exist anywhere in the universe outside of earth. Even on earth, dividing species neatly into "male" and "female" individuals is not always the case. Many species, snails and earthworms, for example, are hermaphroditic and *any* two individuals can mate to produce offspring. Plants are described as having "male" and "female" components, but this certainly is an anthropomorphism that transfers mammalian characteristics onto the vegetable kingdom. As far as extraterrestrial life, we have no clue how any of it may reproduce. There could be advanced asexual organisms, or perhaps tri-sexual reproduction where it took three individuals of three different sexes to produce offspring. Simply put, assuming that "male" and "female" are universal (let alone Divine) attributes is ludicrous.

Literalists like to say "God made Adam and Eve, not Adam and Steve." Well, look carefully at the story. If the point had been that Eve, and not Steve, was the ideal companion over whom Adam would finally celebrate, then Steve would have been introduced to Adam along with the animals. Then Adam could have rejected Steve as the ideal companion at the same time he rejected the dog, cat, cow, sheep, aardvark, and zebra. But that's not how the story is. The story tells of God taking a rib from Adam and making another human being, the only other human being, and there the magic began. To read more into that story is *not* to be faithful to Scripture. The Scripture simply doesn't say that Adam rejoiced over Eve's femaleness or rejected Steve's maleness.

Sodom and Gomorrah (Genesis 19:1-29)

Unfortunately, historical misinterpretation has allowed the term *sodomy* to be fixed erroneously in our vocabularies. Regardless of the exact details (whether only male homosexual acts, or various heterosexual acts, qualify for the modern legal definition), the term as used in colloquial and legal language is misdefined. The basic sin of Sodom was not a sexual one, but one of breaching hospitality. Properly speaking, a "sodomite" should be any person who is not open and accepting of another. Funny how much that sounds like some fundamentalists and homophobic radicals are the true "sodomites."

The story is rather straightforward. God decides to destroy Sodom and Gomorrah because of their "wickedness." God sends two angels disguised as men to the city, and Abraham's nephew Lot greeted the angels and offered them hospitality. The "men" of Sodom demand that Lot let out the angels that they might "know" them. Lot offered them his daughters instead because "the men are under the protection of my roof." The men of Sodom refused. The angels took control, Lot fled, and Sodom was destroyed in fire.

Many hints of homosexuality do arise, but there are serious problems with interpreting homosexual transgressions as the basic sin of Sodom. First, God had decided to destroy the city *before* the angels were sent, so the specific act of what the men wanted to do with the angels was obviously not the reason for the destruction. Second, it is not absolutely clear that *know* meant "to have sex with," although this is certainly a possible interpretation. Third, it is not clear whether the "men" of Sodom included just the males, or all of its citizens, both male and female, in the generic sense of "men," so it is not at all clear that sexual impropriety, if that was what was intended at all, would have been solely homosexual. (So if the story of Sodom and Gomorrah is taken as a blanket condemnation of all homosexual activity, one must at least raise the logical question of whether it should be taken as a blanket condemnation of all heterosexual activity as well.) Fourth, if "know" did refer to sexual acts, they would have been rape, and worse yet the rape of an angel representing God. And finally, Lot's own excuse for not presenting the angels was because they were his guests. He did not argue that they were males or angels,[14] but guests, and that it would be better to abuse his daughters, as horrible as that is, than his guests.

It is very hard for us to understand this obsession with hospitality. (Perhaps someday in the future it will be equally hard for someone looking back at our culture to understand our obsession with sexuality.) We must remember that Abraham, Lot, and all the people of Genesis were nomadic people in a very harsh desert. Not putting a stranger up when he knocked on your door could mean death to the stranger, and there was not a Holiday Inn around the corner. It was simply a different society than ours, with different dangers, different responsibilities, and different moral issues arising out of those dangers and responsibilities.

Finally, Scripture continually uses Sodom as an example of a sinful people, but it does not equate that sin with homosexuality or anything else sexual in nature. Ezekiel 16:49 says, "The crime of your sister Sodom was pride, gluttony, calm complacency." Jesus Himself connects Sodom with inhospitality: "But whenever you enter a town and they do not make you welcome, ... it will be more bearable for Sodom than for that town." (Luke 10:10-12)

Most tragically, the erroneous association of Sodom with homosexuality played a deeply troubling – an thoroughly immoral – role in Western history. While the Bible itself does not directly associate Sodom or Gomorrah with homosexuality, by the time of Christ this

---

[14] This raises another interesting question as to whether angels have any gender at all. It would seem that as purely spiritual creatures, they, like God, are genderless – neither male nor female, neither feminine nor masculine, regardless of the fact that gendered human pronouns may be used for them (as they are for God Who is both genderless and asexual).

association had been made by prominent Jewish writers such as Philo of Alexandria (20 BC – AD 58) and Titus Flavius Josephus (Yosef ben Matiyahu, AD 37-100).

The Christian emperor Justinian I (Flavius Petrus Sabbatus Justinianus Agustus, AD 482-565) directly associated Sodom with "luxuries against nature," *i.e.* homosexual sex, in his laws, the *Corpus Iuris Civilis*.[15]

By coincidence, but making matters far worse, the erath experienced its worst and coldest year in AD 535-36, with summertime snow and famine from Ireland to China and even drought in Peru. Modern science tells us that a dust cloud either from a volcanic eruption or space debris caused this phenomenon. Justinian, however, equated it with the story of Sodom's destruction and blamed it on "sodomy." Thus *sodomia* was coined as a legal term and took on its modern – and erroneous – meaning.

Sadly, Justinian's association perpetuated itself and was vigorously revived nearly 1,000 years later. While dealing with the horrors of the Plague, both religious and civil authorities searched in vain for underlying causes, not having yet discoverd the bacteria and viruses associated with communicable diseases. Clergy and reulers alike often blamed "sodomy," which of course was commonly practiced in medieval and Renaissance times as it always has been throughout mammalian history. This was "homophobia" in the truest sense of the word – a drastic, irrational, unquenchable fear of homosexuals.

Drastic laws were written and sometimes cruelly enforced based on the belief that homosexual acts would not just bring damnation to the culprits, but would bring God's vengeance and destruction to the entire city or state. "Sodomy" became worse than murder because it brought the threat of mass destruction and annihilation to guilty and innocent alike.

Of course history demonstrated no such correlation, but this did not end the paranoia about "sodomy." The severe punishments were not consistently enforced, but this was more

---

[15] *Novela CXLI, <u>Edictum Iustiniani ad Constantinopolitanos de Luxuriantibus Contra Naturam</u>, Caput I. "Scimus enim ex sacris scripturis edocti, quale deus iustum supplicium iis qui Sodomis olim habitarunt, propter hunc in commixtione furorem intulerit, adeo ut in hunc usque diem regio illa inextincto igni ardeat, cum deus per hoc nos erudiat, ut impiam istam actionem aversemur."* Of course Justinian's error is twofold. Homosexuality most certainly is not *"contra naturam,"* being ubiquitous in the animal kingdom, and *sacris scripturis* do <u>not</u> *edocti* (teach) that Sodom was destroyed for acts that were *"contra naturam,"* regardless of what that phrase may mean.

due to the prevalence of the acts and their ability to infiltrate all socioeconomic strata than to any logical effort to evaluate causation of the Plague or any other disaster.

Thus it is the misinterpreted story of Sodom and Gomorrah, regardless of its original intent or interpretation, that has caused homosexuality to be viewed as particularly troublesome and left us with a commonly understood but entirely meaningless term in most modern languages.

And lest we give too much credit to modern understanding, we cannot forget that mere decades ago – not millennia or even centuries – there was a similar mass hysteria surrounding AIDS, in spite of relatively quick identification of the specific virus that causes it and effective ways of inhibiting its transmission. And just as I am writing this in June 2013 the news media was announcing that the FBI's "10 Most Wanted List" now had its 500th person added – a university professor wanted for travelling internationally to have sex with 14-year-olds that he had met on the internet. Really? One of the 10 most wanted people in the world, on the same list that had Osama bin Laden? Within the same five minutes on the radio we heard about a man who had just killed his ex-wife. Shouldn't he be more wanted? Isn't he more dangerous? Or the ones we heard about the day before, a man and woman who had so abused their baby that the one-year-old baby died. The teenagers are still alive (and probably still soliciting sex). The ex-wife and the baby are dead. The stigma of Sodom and Gomorrah live on.

The true tragedy and really bad theology of the Sodom story, of course, is that people buy into the idea that God would have destroyed a city for any reason. It doesn't matter what the reason might have been – gay sex, straight sex, group sex, rape, sex with angels, being rude to strangers, disobeying the rules of desert hospitality, or even flagrant idolatry for that matter. The idea that God would have destroyed the city for _any_ reason is simply false. That is simply not how God acts. That concept is something inherited from prescientific times when everything, good or bad, human-caused or nature-caused, was credited or blamed on a god. The ancient Hebrews were no different in that matter, but just because the God they credited or blamed was the True God doesn't mean their credit or blame were true. God no more destroyed Sodom and Gomorrah than Zeus flings down lightning bolts. We _must_ put that concept to rest in the dust heap of ancient errors, regardless of how it is recorded in the

Bible! We cannot really claim to be Christian – followers of the God of Love – and still believe such things. Sodom was destroyed by a natural disaster, nothing more.

The Holiness Code (Leviticus 18:22 and 20:13)

Unlike all other supposed references to homosexuality in Scripture, these two passages from Leviticus are the only ones that clearly discuss male-male sex. "You shall not have intercourse with a man as you would with a woman. This is an abomination." These verses discuss physical acts, not states of mind, relationships, or internal orientations. It is because of them that some moderates in the Church have concluded that homosexual orientation is acceptable, but that carrying out the actions is sinful. We contend that these moderates are wrong and that the activities themselves are not sinful, even though Leviticus calls them "abominations" and in one place assigns the death penalty.

First, it is important to understand what "abomination" means. The Hebrew word is תעבה *(to`ebah)*. The word deals primarily with ritual impurity. It is used to describe things such as cast idols (Deuteronomy 27:15). Keeping idolatry in mind, it is important to note the ordering of the verses of Leviticus. There is a whole string of prohibitions against incest, followed by prohibition of intercourse with a woman "in a state of menstrual pollution" (18:19). (Yes, this part of the Bible is full of sexist references to the natural menstrual processes as being "unclean" and "disgusting.")

Then (18:21) there is prohibition of what many translations describe as sacrificing children (certainly a form of idolatry), and then the prohibition against homosexuality, which alone of these sexual sins is called *to`ebah*.  Actually, in the verse usually translated to involve child sacrifice, the Hebrew word for what is sacrificed is זרע *zera`*, which is translated as σπερματος *(spermatos)* in the Septuagint, *semine* in the Vulgate, "seed" in the King James Version, and "offspring" in the New Revised Standard Version. There is a certain ambiguity as to whether the term means living infants/children or semen (i.e., potential children), and most discussions on the verse refer to child sacrifices, even though the same word *zera`* is used in the previous verse (18:20) in a way that can only mean "semen." (Modern translations usually read something akin to "You shall not have sexual relations with your kinsman's wife" although the Hebrew literally reads "You shall not give your semen to the wife of your neighbor.") We simply cannot tell for sure whether Leviticus 18:21 is talking about ritualistic infanticide, as was certainly known in some cultures, or some sort of strange ceremony in which the fluid products of masturbation were offered as a burnt sacrifice. Obviously the sacrifice of children would be considered a heinous crime in nearly any modern society while the offering of semen, though perhaps ridiculed and thought of as anything from bizarre to perverse, would most likely be protected in the United States as part of the Constitution's guarantee of religious freedom. We learn at least two key issues from this review: (1) the ancient Hebrews' views on reproduction were not entirely clear given the ambiguity between "semen" and "children,"[16] and (2) the idolatrous religions of the area had clear sexual overtones that seem odd to us today.

As we discussed above, homosexual sex acts (as well as heterosexual) were part of the fertility cult, the local pagan religion that the Hebrews were ordered to stay away from at all cost.

Homosexuality, therefore, was prohibited not because it in and of itself is evil, but because it was, for this culture, in this time and place, part and parcel of the pagan religion. It was *to`ebah*; it was seen as a pagan worship experience which took away from the worship of the True God. Leviticus is not talking about two men in love. Nor is it talking about two men just "playing around" and having a good time. It is talking about participation in a pagan religious ceremony.

This religious practice was unfortunately not distinguished through history and translation from other types of homosexual activity. In various places the Old Testament speaks of the קדשם *qadeshim* (derived from קדש *qadosh*, "holy"), which were the Canaanitic priests of the fertility cult. Some older versions of the Bible unfortunately translate this word as "sodomites" in Deuteronomy 23:17 and various places in First and Second Kings (such as I Kings 14:24). Newer translations usually use a closer term such as "sacred prostitute." In fact many footnotes explain the fertility religion for these chapters, but do not bother to carry

---

[16] At least one common ancient belief was that the full child was contained within the man's semen, the seed, and that the woman was merely the vessel in which the seed was planted. This explains the synonymous relationship between the Latin and Greek words for male semen and the seeds of plants and, for that matter, the fact that the English word for the ejaculatory product is actually the Latin word for the seed of a plant, *semen*, and the English word for the cells that carry male genetic material ("sperm") is derived from the Greek word for the seed of a plant, *spermatos*.

the explanation forward to conclude that understanding the pagan cults is paramount to our understanding of *all* references to either homosexuality or prostitution in the Bible, and perhaps for any understanding of the Bible's perspective on sexuality of any sort. (This relationship with "prostitution" is discussed in much greater detail in the chapter following.)

While we are discussing translations, it is important to be very leery of the way many modern Bibles try to translate *to`ebah*. "Abomination" (King James) actually is not too bad, because the English word has a sort of technical ring and no one knows exactly what it means. "Disgusting" is not quite as good because it conveys an emotional content that is not necessarily applicable. "Hateful thing" and other less literal terms are truly problematic if they imply that God hates a person. God, however, is Pure Love, and hatred is simply *not* part of His Being.

Now, aside from the fact that the "man lying with a man" refers to the idolatrous pagan religious practices, let us assume that we wanted to follow the Levitical law. Fundamentalists seem to think it should apply to homosexuals, so let us carefully explain some of the consequences.

As we have already seen, sex during menstruation is definitely out (Lev 18:19), but if anyone should do it, both the man and woman are to be expelled from the city (Lev 20:18). Any two men who have sex together should both, of course, be put to death (Lev 20:13), but so should any man or woman who is a magician (Lev 20:27) as should any man who commits adultery with his neighbor's wife (Lev 20:10). Oh yes, the wife gets the axe, too. Incest, of course, is a capital crime, so maybe we should ban heterosexuality altogether just to be safe in case you accidentally had heterosexual relations with a person who was an unknown relative. There are, after all, far more verses that deal with heterosexuality than there are that deal with homosexuality.

Enough about sex. You'd better discard your cotton-polyester shirts and blouses because "you must not wear a garment made from two kinds of fabric" (Lev 19:19). And yes, the Jehovah's Witnesses are probably right in choosing to die rather than take a life-saving blood transfusion (Lev 17:12).

Of course we all know that ham and bacon are taboo (Lev 11:7), but you'd better not even touch it when your friend at breakfast asks you to pass the bacon (Lev 11:8). And as for shrimp, lobster, and oysters, certainly you were aware that "whatsoever hath no fins nor scales in the waters, that shall be an abomination unto you." (Lev 11:12, *KJV*).

And don't forget to destroy that priceless Ming vase if you see a spider in it (Lev 11:33) or to take your stove out into the front yard and smash it to bits if a lizard gets on it (Lev 11:35). And finally, you'd better call a rabbi over right away to check out the mildew in your shower, and if it comes back after you clean it, you have to tear down your whole house and haul the rubble away to the toxic waste dump (an "unclean place outside the city") (Lev 14:43-45). And if you are lucky enough to have the mildew disappear, go out and quickly catch two birds so you can kill one and use the live one to dip in the blood of the dead bird and fling it around your mildew-free house. (Lev 14:49-53).

By the way, in case you've lived such a chaste, dietetically pure life in a house with no lizards, spiders, or mildew and therefore think that you're safe, just pray that no one ever heard you yell at your mother that time when you were a kid. "Anyone who curses father or mother will be put to death." (Lev 20:9)

Those Who Rejected God (Romans 1:18-32)

This passage contains the only negative reference to lesbianism in the Bible. (A discussion of a positive reference follows in the next section of this booklet.) In this passage, it is important to note that Paul is specifically talking about people who have chosen to leave the fold of the faithful and enter into idolatrous religions. They "exchanged the glory of the immortal God for an imitation, for the image of a mortal human being, or of birds, or animals, or crawling things." Here he covers much of the paganism found in ancient Rome, Greece, Egypt, and the Middle East.

Among the things he says of these people is that they (men and women) have been abandoned by God to their passions (because they chose to leave God). These passions drove them to "unnatural practices" and homosexual passions. The paragraph itself has a rather bizarre logic. God abandons the people to their passions, which are "unnatural." How they can be both passions that take hold when one is abandoned and "unnatural" is not explained.

Yet this verse is the source of the term "unnatural vice" sometimes used to refer to homosexuality. Science and observation, of course, tell us that homosexual activity is not at all unnatural. Both male and female homosexuality are rather routinely observed in nature, among mammals and other animals who practice it either on occasion or routinely. Most gay people, as well as psychologists and psychiatrists, will point out that homosexuality is deeply rooted in the emotional nature of gay individuals. Their "nature" therefore is homosexual.

Paul, of course, had a significantly different concept of "nature" (φυσιν [*physin*] in Greek) than most modern people do. It is not fair to take our concepts and put them back on Paul's words. Paul said that long hair on a man is unnatural, but is part of nature for a woman (I Corinthians 10:11-12). Yet surely Paul was aware of the Nazirites of the Old Testament (Numbers 6). They were somewhat like monks, and one of their vows was not to cut their hair. Their long hair was a sign of their vows and of their strength. (Samson was a Nazirite.) Likewise, Paul must have been aware that hair grew naturally long on males (as well as females), otherwise there would be no need to cut it.

Paul also uses "nature" to describe qualities that are circumstantial (but not genetic) by birth, as in Galatians 2:15 where some are called "Jews by nature." Certainly if one could be Jewish by nature, psychology would tell us that one could also be homosexual by nature. In this case, "those who exchanged what is natural for the unnatural" would include those intrinsically homosexual persons who chose to enter into heterosexual relationships for the sake of society, religion, or other unnatural reasons. Unfortunately this is a rather large group of people. Worse yet, the Church is at least partially responsible for much of this dishonesty.

The bottom line with Romans 1 is that Paul was primarily discussing persons who have abandoned Christianity for paganism. Among the things they do, obviously, is participate in the pagan rituals, many of which were homosexual in nature (others were heterosexual, and many, of course, were not sexual). The main focus of Romans 1 is not sexuality, but abandoning true religion. How ironic it is that some supposed followers of Jesus use Romans 1 to make Christianity seem so intolerable that they cause would-be believers to abandon it.

The Lists of "No-No's" (I Corinthians 6:9; I Timothy 1:10)

These verses represent mistranslation at its worst. Of all the scriptural passages dealing with sexuality, these lists of words are the most dangerous because it is so easy to add one's personal thoughts into a translation, particularly with words that are very obscure.

The Greek list is πορνοι, ειδωλολατραι, μοιχοι, μαλακοι, αρσενοκοιται, κλεπται, πλεονεκται, μεθυσοι, λοιδοροι, and άρπαγες, or in our alphabet, *pornoi, eidōlolatrai, moichoi, malakoi, arsenokoitai, kleptai, pleonektai, methusoi, loidoroi*, and *harpages*. The first five will be our primary concern, but we should not ignore the last five, as this will put the whole thing in perspective. The last five all have to do with interactions with other people and can be translated:

κλεπται	*kleptai*	thieves
πλεονεκται	*pleonektai*	coveters
μεθυσοι	*methusoi*	drunkards
λοιδοροι	*loidoroi*	revilers
άρπαγες	*harpages*	plunderers[17]

The first five are related to idolatry and paganism, although most people get distracted into thinking that they have to do with sex. While Paul no doubt had sexual connotations in mind, the main point is not the sexual acts themselves, but the idolatrous nature of the sex.

Πορνοι (*pornoi*) is usually translated "fornicators," "sexually immoral," or some other technically meaningless term. "Prostitutes" is a better translation, but then it is important to remember that we meant the cultic prostitutes and *not* the classic American streetwalker. Ειδωλολατραι (*eidōlolatrai*) means "idolaters." It is important to note that this word is placed right in the middle of the list of supposedly sexual words! Μοιχοι (*moichoi*) means "adulterers" and is derived from the word for "impurity." Remember, though, that adultery in the Bible is intimately connected with idolatry and is often used as a symbol for the latter, far more serious sin.

---

[17] The Vulgate translation of *harpages* is *rapaces*, which means "robbers" or "plunderers," but is also the root of the English word *rape*. It is curious that English Bible translators never translate this word as "rapists."

The fourth and fifth words, μαλακοι (*malakoi*) and αρσενοκοιται (*arsenokoitai*), are the two that are usually misused to refer to homosexuality. *Malakoi* technically means "soft ones" and is sometimes used as a euphemism for the morally weak. The King James Bible translators translated it as "effeminate," and this mistaken translation has permeated many other works. *Arsenokoitai* is a very rare Greek word used twice by Paul and only once or twice else in all extant ancient Greek literature. It is derived from the words for "male" and "bed," but it is certainly not the common Greek word used to refer to participants in homosexual activity. Some English Bibles translate it as "homosexuals," others specifically make it the insertive partners (with *malakoi* supposedly being the receptive partners). Others simply render the two terms together as "homosexuals."

This, of course, begs the question as to why Paul did not use the common ancient Greek words for "active" (δρωτες [*drōntes*] and παιδερατα [*paideratai*]) and "passive" (πασχοντες [*paschontes*] and παιδικα [*paidika*]) homosexual participants. The most credible explanation is that *malakoi* and *arsenokoitai*, like *pornoi* and *moichoi*, were somehow intimately connected with idolatry, not family arrangements or lifestyles, and that Paul's immediate audience would have known this and made the distinctions.[18]

An equally important question, of course, is why the self-appointed custodians of modern morality make such a big issue out of the *arsenokoitai* and ignore the *kleptoi*. Most all of us are guilty of a little kleptomania. Would Jerry Falwell, Lou Sheldon, or Fred Phelps[19] really argue that someone who makes a personal telephone call from work or eats a piece of candy while walking around in the store will not enter the Kingdom of Heaven? Should kleptomaniacs by the same logic be denied basic rights in housing and employment? Should the marriage of two kleptomaniacs be considered legal? After all, the *kleptoi* are in the very same list as the *arsenokoitai*, and we even know what *kleptoi* means!

---

[18] As later in this work we will show that the early Church certainly did not interpret these words as referring to the homosexual pairing that was the norm in that culture.

[19] Jerry Falwell was a fundamentalist Baptist televangelist and founder of the so-called "Moral Majority," a now-defunct national foundation promoting his moralistic views. Lou Sheldon is a free-lance minister located in Anaheim, California, who heads the so-called "Traditional Values Coalition" and stirs up hatred whenever a state or local government tries to legislate nondiscrimination or equal marriage rights. Fred Phelps is a fanatic in Kansas who, with some members of his family, tours the United States picketing funerals and other disgusting acts pretending to stand for "Biblical" views of homosexuality.

Gay Love in the Bible

Two Bible stories must be related in light of this discussion of homosexuality in the Bible. They are beautiful stories that are sadly overlooked.

Naomi and Ruth

> "Wherever you go, I shall go,
> wherever you live, I shall live.
> Your people will be my people,
> and your God will be my God."

We've all heard these words. They even make little necklace charms with this verse on them and then cut the charm in two. Sometimes they make the stupid mistake of making one charm bigger than the other, as if one would be worn by a man and one by a woman. How strange, since the words (Ruth 1:16) were said by one woman to another.

Naomi was Ruth's mother-in-law. Naomi had two sons. Her husband died. Her sons married, and then they, too, died. Naomi was left with her two daughters-in-law, Orpah and Ruth. All three were widows.

Orpah and Ruth were Moabites. When her sons died, Naomi thought it would be best for Orpah and Ruth if they went back to Moab. Orpah did; Ruth refused. Ruth and Naomi spent the rest of their lives together. Ruth married again, and Naomi adopted her new husband. She was the grandmother of King David, and hence an ancestor of Jesus.

Whether or not Ruth and Naomi were lesbian lovers is not discussed. It would not have been much of an issue because the sexist society of their time did not pay much attention to what women did with each other.

The story is, however, certainly one of love, dedication, and commitment. It is beautiful to see how these women took care of each other through their lives.

David and Jonathan

King David certainly had an interesting life filled with many military, political, and sexual adventures. It is tragic that if asked who the real love of David's life was, most people would probably answer "Bathsheba." For some reason David's affair with this wife of one of his soldiers, and the conniving murder of her husband in order to add her to his harem, has even caught the attention of Sunday School children.

Yet David himself answers the question for us:

> "Jonathan, by your dying I too am stricken,
> I am desolate for you, Jonathan my brother.
> Very dear you were to me,
> your love more wonderful to me
> than the love of a woman."

Why should we not believe David for his own words? Jonathan (who was not David's brother, but his best friend and lover) was the son of King Saul. This is the lament of David recorded in II Samuel 1:25-26. David makes it clear that Jonathan was the one person in all the world that he loved the most. What more evidence do we need? David said Jonathan's love was better than the love of a woman, and David certainly had enough women to know what he was talking about. It is only the blinded eye of homophobia that cannot see through this wonderful love story.

The First Book of Samuel is intertwined with the story of David and Jonathan. In the 18th chapter, David has just been introduced to King Saul after killing Goliath. We read, "Jonathan felt an instant affection for David; Jonathan loved him like his very self ... Jonathan made a pact with David, since he loved him like his very self." (I Sam 18:1-5).

Saul brought David into his household, and he eventually married Saul's daughter Michal. As David's military might developed, Saul became jealous and tried to kill him. Jonathan interceded repeatedly on David's behalf, finally to the point that Saul would not tell his own son and confidant of his plans to destroy David (I Sam 20:3). In fact, Saul finally became enraged with his son because he knew that Jonathan's primary loyalty was to David, not to his father and king. "Don't I [Saul] know that you [Jonathan] side with the son of Jesse [David] to your own shame and your mother's dishonor!" (I Sam 20:30).[20]

Jonathan strategized to save David from Saul's wrath. After the plan worked, Jonathan and David met in the fields, "and they kissed one another, and wept one with another, until David exceeded." (I Sam 20:41). "Until David exceeded" is a strange appendage that consistently plagues translators. The word is הגביל, *higdiyl*, and many translations use a footnote that says "Hebrew uncertain." The Hebrew is an emphatic form of גבל, *gadol*, "to be large," "to grow up," or "to exceed." There is evidence from other ancient writings that this term was a slang euphemism for "orgasm," similar to the English slang use of the word *come*.

The evidence is quite clear that David and Jonathan were lovers. The Bible is full of the story. The love story of David and Jonathan is as clearly portrayed as any other biblical love story. All we need to do is remove the blindfolds of bias and read the story for what it says.

This leaves, of course, two questions: "Could it really have happened?" and "Why wasn't it condemned by the same moralistic narrative that condemned David for his murder of Bathsheba's husband?"

The answer to the first question is absolutely "Yes." Male-male relationships between upper-class men, such as Jonathan, son of the king, and common people, such as David the shepherd boy, were frequent in the ancient Near East. It was an accepted part of the culture. In fact, although the biblical narrative does not specifically state it, it is quite possible that the reason that David originally entered the household of Saul as his musician is because Jonathan had brought him home as his new lover. This would explain Saul's keen awareness of Jonathan's loyalty to David, even over and above his loyalty to his own father Saul. This relationship would *not* have been viewed as unusual or distasteful.

It also should be noted that such relationships in the ancient Near East (as also the case with homosexuality in ancient Greece) did not preclude heterosexual relationships, whether they be for the sake of love, politics, or procreation. The concept of an exclusively gay lifestyle was unknown, or at least uncommon. Because procreation was such an important goal in the world at that time (when the population was miniscule compared with today),

---

[20] Presumably Jonathan's mother was dishonored only because in that sexist society a woman's primary role was to produce a loyal son.

exclusive homosexual relationships were very rare. Even deeply loving and committed male lovers would also have heterosexual partners. (Remember, of course, that most wealthy men in that culture were also polygamous, so their whole concept of marriage, including the idea that a woman would have any sort of exclusive relationship with her husband, was radically different than ours.)

Finally, the relationship between Jonathan and David was not condemned by the moralists because it was not seen as immoral, any more than David's harem *per se* was seen as immoral. (Remember, David got in trouble for killing Bathsheba's husband, not for taking her as one more woman of his harem.) Clearly David was not breaking the spirit of the levitical law. His relationship with Jonathan had nothing to do with the fertility cults, and so it was not condemned.

The Centurion and His Boy/Slave

In many Eucharistic liturgies, after the prayer of consecration and before the communion of the faithful, the priest lifts the Host and says, "This is the Lamb of God Who takes away the sins of the world. Happy are those who are called to His Supper." The faithful then respond, "Lord, I am not worthy to receive You, but only say the word and I shall be healed." In the Roman Catholic English rite of 2011 the response was made, "Lord, I am not worthy that you should enter under my roof, but only say the word and my soul shall be healed." The Italian Roman Catholic Mass has "*O Signore, non sono degno di partecipare alla tua mensa, ma di' soltanto una parola e io sarò salvato.*" The Spanish has *"Señor, no soy digno de que entres en mi casa, pero una palabra tuya bastará para sanarme."*

These are all paraphrases of what a Roman centurion said to Jesus in one of the stories of healing recorded in Matthew 8:5-13 and Luke 7:1-10. In Matthew the centurion himself was talking to Jesus but did not feel it necessary that Jesus actually come to his house, rather that Jesus had sufficient authority to merely pronounce healing by word, much as the centurion himself was accustomed to giving orders and being obeyed. He thus said to Jesus, "*Kyrie, ouk eimi ikanos hina mou hupo tēn stegēn eiselthēs, alla monon eipe logō, kai iathēstai ho pais mou.*" That is literally, "Lord (*Kyrie*), I am not worthy that You might come under my roof (*stegēn*),[21] but only say the word (*logos*) and my boy (*pais*) will be healed." The story in Luke is essentially the same, although it has Jewish friends of the centurion approach Jesus and say these words for him.

Most commentaries and sermons on these passages focus on the centurion's faith and Jesus' healing ability. Our key question, however, is "Who exactly was it that was healed?" The answer lies in three Greek words used to describe the sick person. Neither one of the two nouns alone is sufficient to discern exactly the relationship between the centurion and the man who was healed by Jesus. However, used together they speak volumes.

Both Matthew and Luke use παις (*pais*) in the statement made by the centurion (or on his behalf) with reference to Jesus visiting his house. This word means "boy." In Greek it had many of the denotations and connotations that it has in English. Literally, of course, it meant "son" or "child," though the specific Greek word for "son" is υιος (*huios*), the term used to describe Jesus's relationship with God the Father. *Huios* is also used in the same Matthew passage (8:12) to describe the Jews as the *huioi tē Basileia*, "sons of the Kingdom."

Pais was also sometimes used to refer to a servant. This is not unlike the way male slaves were sometimes called "boy" in the slave-holding regions of the United States before the Civil War.[22] *Pais* also could refer to the younger man who was the lover of an older adult man in the classical Greek arrangement of gay love, similar to the way "boy" is sometimes used within the modern gay community[23] or, for that matter, the way it is used in the English word "boyfriend" whether in a homosexual or heterosexual context. Thus from this word alone it is not clear whether Jesus healed the centurion's son, servant, or lover. English Bibles typically translate the word as "servant."

In Luke we encounter the dual-word complication (for those who want to deny that the Bible says anything positive about homosexuality) or the clarification. Remember, the story in Luke has some Jews speaking on behalf of the centurion, whereas Matthew has the centurion himself talking with Jesus. The Jews in the Luke story tell Jesus that the centurion has a δουλος (*doulos*) that is sick and dying, specifying that this particular *doulos* was εντιμος

---

[21] Hence the Stegosaurus, the "roof lizard" because of the plates on its back.

[22] A reason why the term, when used by a white person to address a black man, is considered derogatory and racist.

[23] It is, of course, the root of the English word "pederasty."

(*entimos*) by the centurion. The Jews go into elaborate detail as to why this particular centurion was a supporter of Israel and thus worthy of this healing transaction. Interestingly, when they quote the centurion's words to Jesus, they tell Him that the centurion's *pais* is ill.

Doulos is the word for "slave." In spite of modern views on the subject, slavery was common in Jesus's time and culture and was not (much to our chagrin) condemned by the Bible. (The same is true of what we today would call "pederasty.") Because slavery was so common and condoned, one wonders if the Jewish messengers were trying to avoid using the potentially more "controversial" concept of the centurion's *pais*. Nonetheless, the combined use of the two words, together with the adjective *entimos*, seems to make it clear that the person healed could only have been the centurion's lover.

One would never refer to a son or daughter as a "slave," so this virtually lets out the possibility that the centurion was talking about his biological child. Likewise, slaves typically were property and were not usually *entimos*, which means "esteemed" or "highly honored" and derives from τιμη (*timē*), "honor" or "price." While it could mean a slave that was particularly valuable (*i.e.*, worth a lot of money) or useful (*i.e.*, a very good worker), the efforts to which the centurion went, together with his use of *pais*, make it very unlikely that he was merely trying to have Jesus save a valuable asset. The *New Revised Standard Version* somewhat misses the point with its translation "had a slave whom he valued highly." The *New Jerusalem Bible*'s translation is much more subtle and carries the nuances of the Greek, "had a servant, a favourite of his." The British spelling of "favourite" helps remind us that this term is a common euphemism for "lover" in British English.

The centurion himself did not view the words *pais* and *doulos* as mere synonyms. In the Matthew passage he explains to Jesus that he is used to giving orders and having them carried out by his *stratiōtoi* ("soldiers") and *douloi*, yet it is his *pais* that he wishes Jesus to heal. Based on the combination of all these words in the story, the only really viable relationship between the centurion and the one Jesus healed is that of lover. This would have been a common occurrence among Roman military men of the time, so in that respect, it is not surprising.

Likewise, it is not unusual that the same word for "slave" could also mean "lover." Remember in this culture wives were considered property and teenage girls were often purchased from their fathers or from slave traders. It was also common for men to similarly purchase their young male lovers, either from families or slave dealers. One might do well to recall that Jacob purchased his two wives from his uncle (by working for him) and that the twelve tribes of Israel descended from these two women as well as each of their slaves (four women in total).

The important point, of course, is that Jesus responded and healed the *pais*. He did not lecture the centurion on Levitical law. He did not discuss the destruction of Sodom and Gomorrah. Instead, He not only healed the centurion's "boy," but went on to use the centurion's faith as an example to the Jews. One can easily then grasp the power of this story. A centurion – not only a non-Jew, but an officer of the Roman army, and one with a male lover at that – has faith that is greater than many of the children of Israel.

Thus this paragon of faith, whom we all paraphrase at every Mass, was a gay (or bisexual) Gentile soldier.

Prostitution and "Fornication"

A New Outlook

This section was added in the fifth edition (2013) as we realized that what the Bible says about prostitution is just as misunderstood as what it says about homosexuality, and for similar reasons. Furthermore, unlike the numerous volumes that have been printed to clarify the Bible's true discussion (or lack thereof) of homosexuality, little has been done regarding prostitution. Thus the mitigation of the moral stigma against homosexuals has done little if anything to eliminate a similar stigma against sex workers.

Sadly, the evolution of modern views regarding sexuality reflects this as well. Homosexual acts have been decriminalized in the civilized world. The legal rights of gay and lesbian married couples continue to expand. Yet at the same time prostitution – even between fully consenting, free adults – remains a crime in many, if not most, places. Legal prostitution is an anomaly limited to rural counties of Nevada (and contrary to both common belief and actual practice, not Las Vegas) and a few other specific locales in the world.

In fact, it remains widely accepted that prostitution is always "wrong." The logic behind such beliefs is difficult to follow. Why would a person who accepts casual sex between consenting adults think it suddenly became wrong if money were exchanged? And how is a negotiated payment of cash different than buying dinner and a movie?

Surely misinterpretation of the Bible is one of the primary sources of this rational inconsistency, just as it has been with regard to homosexuality. For whatever reason – perhaps the political clout of gays versus prostitutes, or perhaps the fact that homosexuality is an innate part of vertebrate nature and the personal consistency of a significant proportion of specific individuals while prostitution is (for many at least) a free choice of careers – little has been done to rectify this misinterpretation of the Biblical views of prostitution.

To some extent, even the scholarly research and works to mitigate the anti-homosexual views have reinforced the anti-prostitution views. This is, in part, caused by the term "sacred prostitute" or any of its synonyms – "temple prostitute," "cult prostitute," etc. The use of the term "prostitute," even with its religious modifiers, to translate *qadesh* and *qadeshah* causes a mental association with modern sex workers and puts them both into a common category. The condemnations of the *qadesh* and *qadeshah* are thus easily translated into condemnations against the entire category of "prostitutes." In the same way that translating these terms as "sodomite" or "effeminate" unfairly leads to condemnation of gays and/or other gender identities, so this association with sex workers is equally unfair. The terms "sex-priest" and "sex-priestess" are better translations for this reason.

Regardless of the specific types of sex-priest and regardless of the specific types of prostitute, they are all radically different from each other in terms of purpose. As with most of the moral issues of the Bible, it is the *purpose*, not the act itself, that determines its moral character. Killing your own cow to eat it is morally quite different than killing a neighbor's cow for the sake of revenge.

We can envision many types of modern prostitute. These may range from the entirely free adult who chooses to supplement his or her income by charging for sexual favors. This could be a massage therapist who gives "happy endings," an escort who accompanies a client on dates with the agreed assumption that it will be followed by sex, a person who advertises sexual favors on the internet, or any number of other variations. At the other extreme it could be a child who has essentially been kidnapped or held hostage and forced to perform sexual favors for the benefit of the kidnapper or pimp. The moral implications of these two extremes are clearly different, but the difference is not one of sexual acts but of free choice.

We will learn that many of the non-religious sex workers of Roman times were indeed slaves forced by their owners to provide sexual services not by their choice or for their benefit, but for the financial gain of their owners. In fact the word "prostitute" and its Latin cognate *prostituta* come from *pro-statuere*, "to stand out front" because the slaves were forced to stand in front of the brothel to attract clients. Just as we must be careful with Biblical statements about the sex-priests, we also must be careful with the (relatively few) Biblical statements about the slave-prostitutes. Neither of them represents the modern escort or even most "call-girls," "rent-boys," or "hookers."

Just as there are many types of modern sex workers, so it is likely that there were many types of *qadeshim* and *qadeshot*, sex-priests and sex-priestesses. There is ample evidence of their existence in Old Testament times, both in the Bible and in numerous other contemporary writings. However, their exact purposes, functions, activities, and roles may in fact be permanently lost to history. It is particularly problematic to draw generalizations from ancient writings even when those writing share details. That would be akin to generalizing the acts and desires of all modern sex workers based upon the writing or description of a particular escort or hooker.

Much has been written about the sex-priests in recent times (mostly referring to them as some sort of "prostitute") but many of those authors have agendas that narrow their discussions.[24] Some, for example, attempt to tout the value of having a "female" goddess (as opposed to only "male" deities)[25] and discuss the roles that the female sex-priestess played but neglect or minimize the roles of the male sex-priests or assume that they are eunuchs playing essentially "feminine" roles (much as St. Jerome used the term *effeminatus*). Others try to incite homophobic disgust and negatively emphasize the physical acts of the male sex-priests. Some assume that the female sex-priestesses only served male worshippers and that the male sex-priests only served female worshippers. Others assume the male sex-priests were always the receptive party to male worshippers. Some talk of them being in temples. Other stories have them walking on the street. Some speak of the duty of every girl to serve as a sex-priestess once and only once prior to her marriage. Others speak of the *hieros-gamos*, the "sacred marriage" where the king and the sex-priestess consummated a symbolic human-divine marriage. Some discuss the worshippers choosing which one to have sex with, the less attractive taking longer to have their vows fulfilled. Others speak of them being veiled and unseen by the worshipper. Some of them accepted payment, others did not.

All of these variances probably occurred. Today there is tremendous variety in Christian worship (let alone differences between different religions) even though there is also a great deal of similarity that permeates them all. There is no reason to assume that the pagan sex rituals were any less likely to show variety.

---

[24] We, too, of course have an agenda, which is to show that the Bible does not generically condemn either homosexuality or prostitution. We pray that our agenda is neither hidden nor clouds our discussion.

[25] The words "female" and "male" are in quotes because they are attributes of terrestrial animal life that cannot be truly assigned to gods or goddesses, even pagan ones.

We must also remember that all of our knowledge comes through about three thousand years of cultural change. Not only are the available resources in an old (and perhaps extinct) language, but words slowly change meaning through time. Translators – even those with no ulterior motive – may simply miss the point. Imagine, for example, someone a thousand years from now, in the 31st century, reading several novels in which an adult woman has sexual relations with her "boyfriend." Let's assume that the word "boyfriend" has come out of usage and that lovers are no longer called "boyfriends" or "girlfriends." Now assume that this reader learns that the term "cougar" not only refers to the feline puma, but also to a woman who has sex with a much younger man. Although the reader has only found one extant book in which a woman is called a "cougar," the 31st century reader concludes that the vast majority of women of the 21st century were cougars because they so frequently talk about "boyfriends," and "boy" is clearly the term for a young male. Words change. What exactly a *qadesh* or a *qadeshah* – a "holy one" – was we may never know. But it does not matter.

The important thing is that they were all idolatrous – not because they involved acts of sex, but because they involved worship of other gods. *This is why they were condemned.* It is simply not important what they did, how they did it, with whom they did it, what god or goddess they served, or what that god or goddess allegedly received from the cultic sex. The point is that they were part of the pagan idolatry which directly contravened the developing monotheism. This evolution in human understanding of God had little to do with sex, positively or negatively. It had to do with learning new ways of appeasing God and, most important of all, learning that there was only one God. Thus serving other gods or goddesses – whether through sex or any other mechanism – was the number one moral affront of the day.

Although this is cloudy in our eyes today, it was perfectly clear to the original audience of the Old Testament writers.

"Sodomites," Prostitution, and Premarital Sex

It may seem strange to lump these together, but I do it because of their common linguistic roots. As we discussed early in this book, the Greek word πορνεια (*porneia*) is the root from which we get our word *fornication* (as well as *pornography*, which means "writing of a prostitute.") Through the ages, "fornication" has somehow come to mean sex outside of marriage or, more specifically, premarital sex. *Porneia* means "prostitution" in Greek.

The steps were simple over the course of 2,000 years. A Greek word was incorporated into English. The English word was given a new meaning. People then thought the Greek word got a new meaning, and they put that new meaning into the mouths of the writers of the Bible. Whatever that is, it is *not* being true to Scripture.

The Bible does not discuss "fornication." The word and its modern meanings were unknown. (The acts were known, but the word *porneia* didn't refer to them and there was no specific word that had the generic sense of the modern "fornication.") The noun has a verb form πορνευω, *porneuō*, which basically means "to have sex with a prostitute." This verb was translated in the Latin Vulgate as *fornicare*, which begins our sad and mistaken journey toward English "fornicate" and Spanish "*fornicar.*"

The connection with "sodomites" is that the Septuagint (the Greek translation of the Old Testament, dating from at least one hundred years before Christ) sometimes translates the Hebrew word *qadesh* as *pornos*. The King James Bible used "sodomite" for this word. As we have discussed above, *qadesh* is from the Hebrew root *QDŠ* meaning "set aside" or "holy," as in the great hymn of Isaiah 6, "*Qadosh, Qadosh, Qadosh*" – "*Sanctus, Sanctus, Sanctus*" – "Holy, Holy, Holy." Clearly by this derivation, the *qadeshim* and *qadeshot* – the male and female "prostitutes" – were associated with religious activities.

There is another Hebrew word, זונה *zonah*, than can mean "prostitute." Its use has less directly religious connotations, though it is often used as a symbol for idolatry or lack of faithfulness in God. For example, Zion is called a *zonah* in Isaiah 1:21.

Let's look at the places where *qadesh* is used in the Hebrew Bible and look at how the word has been translated. Since there are many modern Bible translations, we will provide tables that give the passage, the Hebrew words, the Septuagint (Greek), the Vulgate (Latin), and several English and Spanish versions of the Bible. For the Greek and Latin we will give an approximate direct meaning of the word.

The ten English versions cited:

- The *Douay Bible* [D] (1609), the early English translation of the Vulgate used by Roman Catholics prior to the appearance of modern translations in the 1960s,

- The *King James Version* [KJV] (1611), the early English translation used by Anglicans and Protestants prior to the appearance of modern translations,

- The *New Revised Standard Version* [NRSV] (1989), the primary Bible used for readings in Anglican, Protestant, and Independent Catholic churches;

- The *Revised English Bible* [REB], (1989)

- The *New American Bible* [NAB], (1970), the primary Bible used for readings in Roman Catholic churches,

- The *New Jerusalem Bible* [NJB], (1985), a scholarly translation used by Catholics, Anglicans, and Protestants,

- *Today's English Version* [TEV] ("Good News for Modern Man"), (1978), a modern translation in easy-to-understand English,

- The *New International Version* [NIV], (1978), a translation used by many Evangelicals

- The *New American Standard Bible* [NASB], (1977), another translation used by many Evangelicals,

- and *The Message* [Mes], (2002), a paraphrase in very contemporary English.

Six Spanish versions are cited:

- *La Santa Biblia Antigua Versión de Casiodoro de Reina* (1569, rev 1960) [AVC]

- *La Biblia Latinoamerica* (2005) [BL]

- *Nueva Biblia de Jerusalén* (19750 [NBJ]

- *Dios Habla Hoy* (1979) [DHH]

- *Sagrada Biblia* (traducción de Agustín Magaña Méndez) (2003) [SBM]

- *La Biblia de Nuestro Pueblo* (2009) [BNP].

The Pentateuch

The Pentateuch, the first five books of the Bible, or the so-called "Books of Moses" uses the term *qadesh/qadeshah* five times. In Deuteronomy 23 there is also an interesting juxtaposition of terms giving insight into both the male (*qadesh*) and female (*qadeshah*) versions of the sex-priests and two other terms used for them. The Pentateuch also provides comparison between the Hebrew words *zonah* and *qadeshah*, both often translated as "prostitute."

Genesis 38:21-22 uses the term *qadeshah* three times in a row. They occur within the story of Genesis 38:12-30 which tells how Jacob's son Judah unknowingly had sex with his daughter-in-law Tamar who had tricked him. Tamar was married to Judah's first son, and when he died, she was given to his second son so he could provide heirs for his brother. He practiced coitus interruptus to avoid having children with her and was struck dead for that (God was credited with his death). Since Judah did not provide his third younger son to her, she disguised herself as a *zonah*. Judah met her on the street and negotiated to have sex with her by paying her a goat, and she kept Judah's seal, cord, and staff as collateral until the goat was delivered. She became pregnant, but Judah never realized who she was.

It is then that we first come across the word *qadeshah* in the Bible. Judah's friend goes looking for the woman to deliver the goat and retrieve the collateral. The friend asks where the *qadeshah* was that had been by the road; the people say there has never been a *qadeshah* there, and the friend then goes back and tells Judah that the people said there had never been a *qadeshah* there. The Septuagint consistently translated *qadeshah* as *porne* in all three instances. For reasons long lost, Jerome used three different Latin words in these two verses – *mulier* which means "woman," and *meretrix* and *scortum* which are words for prostitutes. The Douay Bible picked this up, using "woman" in the first instance and "harlot" in the second and third. Most modern Bibles us "temple prostitute" or "shrine prostitute" but sometimes they leave out the modifier and simply use "prostitute" in one or more of the instances.

Later, when it became clear that Tamar was pregnant, Judah was told that his daughter-in-law *zanətah* and was pregnant because of her *zənunim*, Judah ordered her to be burned alive, until she proved that he was the father, at which time he apologized and spared her.

The first verb *zanətah* is often translated as "played the harlot/prostitute/whore" (different versions use different terms). The concluding action that caused her pregnancy, *zənunim*, is sometimes translated as "whoredom" or "harlotry" but sometimes as a generic term such as "misconduct."

Before further discussing the relationship of the words and their translations, it is important to review the story and its consequences. Although Tamar was originally sentenced to death, it was not because she was a prostitute (regardless of the meaning of the words). Judah was perfectly willing to live up to the financial deal trading sex for a goat. It was his daughter-in-law's embarrassing pregnancy – having a child presumably not from his family – that provoked the death penalty. Judah's property (his daughter-in-law) had proven itself unworthy, inadequate, and corrupt, unable to do what it is supposed to do – like a washing machine that no longer cleans clothes and is thereby discarded to the trash. When she demonstrated that the child was of his family – of Judah himself – she was spared. Note also that there was never even any thought of a penalty to Judah for having visited a prostitute, "temple" or otherwise.

So this story clearly conflates the concept of *zonah* and *qadeshah*. Many argue that while it may be true that the *qadeshah* is a pagan priestess, the *zonah* is simply a common prostitute – as this story seems to imply since she was "standing by the roadside," not apparently in some temple. But we cannot know for sure. Tamar had disguised herself, wearing a veil sufficiently substantial that Judah did not recognize his own daughter-in-law (even after having sex with her). In fact, it was "because she had covered her face" that he thought she was a *zonah*. It is not an easy story to envision, either with respect to modern prostitution or with respect to ancient religious practices. Why was it worth a goat to Judah to have sex with a woman he could not even see? Did he view it as some sort of religious offering, perhaps invoking the fertility of his crops? Is the word "temple" misleading for this nomadic period where the people had few if any permanent buildings? Misleading not in the sense that these weren't pagan priests, but that they were indeed wandering among the people, not sitting in a stone temple. Perhaps they were indeed veiled and remained veiled even during sex, since the point was to please the gods, not oneself. We most likely will never know for sure.

The word *zonah* is from the stem *ZNH* that is somewhat obscure but seems to be related to feeding, while the word *qadeshah* is from the stem *QDŠ* that also gives us the words Hebrew word for "holy." Since they clearly refer to the same individual woman (Tamar) in the very same incident, it seems unlikely that the author made any great distinction between a *zonah* and a *qadeshah*. We also know that the Septuagint translated both Hebrew words in this passage as *pornē*.

In Deuteronomy 23:17-19[26] we encounter both the male and female sex priests. The verses might be translated as:

> "None of the daughters of Israel shall be pagan sex-priestesses, and none of the sons of Israel shall be pagan sex-priests. You shall not bring the fee of a sex-priestess or sex-priest into the House of YAHWEH your God as any kind of votive offering; both these things are ritual impurities to YAHWEH your God."

The first two times the words *qadeshah* and *qadesh* are used, the terms derived from "holy" and clearly indicating the religious nature of these people. The Israelites are forbidden from going into this profession. Most modern translations use some variation of "sacred prostitute" for both the females and males. The Douay Bible, following the Vulgate's use of *scortator*, used "whoremonger" for the male which has more of the connotation of a prostitute's client than of a male prostitute. The King James Bible used "sodomite," just as the old Spanish *Antigua Versión de Casiodoro de Reina* (AVC) used "*sodomita*." This unfortunate word choice, not found in Hebrew, Greek, or even Jerome's Latin at this point, perpetuated both the association of Sodom with male-male sex and initiated the future mistranslations of terms for the male sex-priest into generic terms for homosexuals.

In the next verse the terms are *zonah* and *keleb*. As we have discussed, the meaning of *zonah* is less clear as to whether it is cultic or commercial "prostitution." *Keleb* is simply the word for "dog," *i.e.* the house pet, *Canis lupus familiaris*. Dogs were considered "unclean" by the ancient Hebrews, both in the sense of not being edible and not being highly regarded as they are in our culture. (We of course would agree that eating dog is, in fact, "abominable" and "detestable," and this is perhaps an ideal parallel as to what these words mean when used

---

[26] The verses are labeled 17-18 in some versions and 18-19 in others.

in the Bible – not something that is intrinsically immoral[27] but something that just causes an emotional revulsion.)   It appears that *keleb* is a euphemism for a "*qadesh*." The Septuagint and Vulgate left it as "dog," as do many modern translations, though some apply the apparently intended meaning of "sacred prostitute" (which we more correctly translate as "sex-priest").

It is not clear what it means to not bring the wages of a *zonah* or a *keleb* as offerings to God. If no one in the community is allowed to be one, then they would not be earning such wages. Perhaps it more logically meant that one is not to bring money to pay vows to God. Or perhaps it meant that no one is to come to the Israelite priests to appease God through sexual acts.   Clearly a possible meaning is that a commercial prostitute is not to use any of his or her professional profits to pay offerings to God, but that neither appears logical or likely. Again, one should not read too much into the *qadeshah*/*zonah* distinction.

The modern paraphrase Bible *The Message* uses "priest-pimp" to translate *keleb*. This is an innovative, thoughtful, and colorful translation, and we wish that this book had been consistent in using such innovative translations of these terms in other locations. "Sex-priest" is a slightly better translation that "priest-pimp" simply because the male priests themselves were engaging in the religious sexual activity whereas modern pimps are not necessarily sexually involved with their customers.

It is important, while on this subject, to reiterate the concept of the sex-priest which is so foreign to us today. The ancients knew the association between sex and human fertility. They did not necessarily understand plant reproduction, or even the exactly correct mechanisms of human reproduction. They thought of semen as seed (which is what the word means) and probably did not understand that the human female provided the egg. Not knowing how pollen had been involved in making a vegetable seed, and thinking of human sex as planting a seed within a woman, just as one plants a vegetable seed in the ground, the parallels were even more profound in their eyes than in ours. And gods and goddesses were responsible for everything in nature, good and bad. An angry god led to disaster and a happy

---

[27] Certainly most of us think of it as "immoral" to eat dogs or cats, but from a strictly logical sense it is difficult to establish a moral paradigm that makes dog-eating immoral and cow-eating moral; the same can be said not only about the "morality" of pig-eating or shrimp-eating, both forbidden by biblical law, but also about many of the various other practices, including sexual ones, forbidden by biblical law.

god led to good things, but these gods could also be placated by our actions and offerings. Thus sex with a god's representatives would make the god happy and fertile, leading to a good harvest. Hence the sex-priest, the "sacred prostitute," the *qadesh*, the holy one.

"Prostitute" in the Pentateuch (Torah)				
Hebrew	**Septuagint**	**Vulgate**	**English**	**Spanish**
Gen 38:15 זונה *zonah*	πορνην *pornēn*	*meretricem*	harlot [D] harlot [KJV] prostitute [NRSV] prostitute [REB] harlot [NAB] prostitute [NJB] prostitute [TEV] prostitute [NIV] prostitute [Mes]	ramera [AVC] prostituta [BL] ramera [NBJ] prostituta [DHH] prostituta [SBM] prostituta [BNP]
Gen 38:21-22 קדשה *qadeshah*	πορνη *pornē*	*mulier* *meretrix* *scortum*	woman/harlot [D][28] harlot [KJV] prostitute [NRSV] (temple-)prostitute[29] [REB] temple prostitute [NAB] prostitute [NJB] prostitute [TEV] shrine prostitute [NIV] temple prostitute [NASB] prostitute [Mes]	ramera [AVC] prostituta [BL] ramera [NBJ] prostituta [DHH] mujer/prostituta [SBM] ramera [BNP]

---

[28] The word occurs three times in this dialogue. The Vulgate uses *mulier* ("woman") in the first instance, *meretrix* in the second, and *scortum* in the third. *Meretrix* and *scortum* both roughly mean "prostitute." The Douay Bible (an English translation of the Vulgate) uses "woman" in the first instance and "harlot" for the second and third.

[29] Some modern versions use "temple prostitute" consistently, others use "temple prostitute" in the first instance and just "prostitute" later. Other modern versions simply use "prostitute" alone for all three occurrences.

"Prostitute" in the Pentateuch (Torah)				
Hebrew	**Septuagint**	**Vulgate**	**English**	**Spanish**
Gen 38:24a זנתה *zanətah*	εκπεπορνευκεν *ekpeporneuken*	*fornicata est*	hath played the harlot [D] hath played the harlot [KJV] played the whore [NRSV] played the prostitute [REB] played the harlot [NAB] played the harlot [NJB] acting like a whore [TEV] played the harlot [NASB] has been playing the whore [Mes]	ha fornicado [AVC] se ha prostituido [BL] ha fornicado [NBJ] se ha acostado con otros hombres [DHH] se ha portado mal [SBM] se ha prostituido [BNP]
Gen 38:24b זנונים *zənunim*	πορνειας *porneias*	*conburatur* ("ruined" or "burned up")	(not translated) [D] whoredom [KJV] whoredom [NRSV] (not translated) [REB] harloty [NAB] misconduct [NJB] (not translated) [TEV] harlotry [NASB] (pregnant) whore [Mes]	fornicaciones [AVC] (not translated) [BL] de ello (i.e. porque se ha fornicado) [NBJ] de ello (i.e. porque se ha acostado) [DHH] (not translated) [SBM] (not translated) [BNP]

"Prostitute" in the Pentateuch (Torah)

Hebrew	Septuagint	Vulgate	English	Spanish
Dt 23:18 (F)[30] קדשה *qadeshah*	πορνη *pornē*	*meretrix*	whore [D] whore [KJV] temple prostitute [NRSV] temple-prostitute [REB] temple harlot [NAB] sacred prostitute [NJB] temple prostitute [TEV] temple prostitute [NIV] cult prostitute [NASB] sacred prostitute [Mes]	ramera [AVC] prostituta sagrada [BL] hieródula [NBJ] consagrarse a la prositutción pracitcada en cultos paganos [DHH] prostituas sagradas [SBM] consagrarse a la prositutción pracitcada en cultos paganos [BNP]
Dt 23:18 (M) קדש *qadesh*	πορνευων *porneuōn*	*scortator*	whoremonger [D] sodomite [KJV] temple prostitute [NRSV] temple-prostitute [REB] temple prostitute [NAB] sacred prostitute [NJB] temple prostitute [TEV] temple prostitute [NIV] cult prostitute [NASB] sacred prostitute [Mes]	sodomita [AVC] prosituto sagrado [BL] heiródulo [NBJ] *(included with feminine)*[DHH] prostitutos [SBM] *(included with feminine)* [BNP]

---

[30] The word occurs in both its feminine and masculine forms in this verse. "None of the daughters of Israel shall be a *qadeshah*; none of the sons of Israel shall be a *qadesh*."

<table>
<tr><th colspan="5">"Prostitute" in the Pentateuch (Torah)</th></tr>
<tr><th>Hebrew</th><th>Septuagint</th><th>Vulgate</th><th>English</th><th>Spanish</th></tr>
<tr>
<td>Dt 23:19 (female)
זונה
zonah</td>
<td>πορνη
pornē</td>
<td>prostibuli</td>
<td>strumpet [D]
whore [KJV]
prostitute [NRSV]
common prostitute [REB]
harlot [NAB]
prostitute [NJB]
temple prostitute [TEV]
female prostitute [NIV]
harlot [NASB]
sacred whore [Mes]</td>
<td>ramera [AVC]
prostitutas [BL]
prostituta [NBJ]
ese tipo de prostitución [DHH]
prostituta [SBM]
prostituta [BNP]</td>
</tr>
<tr>
<td>Dt 23:19 (male)
כלב
keleb[31]</td>
<td>κυνος
kunos
("dog")</td>
<td>Canis</td>
<td>dog [D]
dog [KJV]
male prostitute [NRSV]
male prostitute [REB]
dog [NAB]
"dog" [NJB–in quotes]
temple prostitute [TEV]
male prostitute [NIV]
dog [NASB]
priest-pimp [Mes]</td>
<td>perro [AVC]
perro [BL]
perro [NBJ]
(included with feminine)[DHH]
prostituto [SBM]
prostituto [BNP]</td>
</tr>
</table>

---

[31] כלב (keleb) is the Hebrew word for "dog" (i.e. the house pet). In this context it appears to be a slang term for a male temple prostitute, though it is tempting, at least facetiously, to take Deuteronomy 23:18 as a prohibition against dog-fighting, not allowing any money earned in such a hideous "sport" to be used to pay Temple obligations. The word is used 32 times in the Hebrew Bible. Of these, 24 clearly refer to canine animals, and only Dt 23:18 is clearly a term for a temple prostitute. Seven other uses, in the books of Samuel, Kings, and Psalms could refer to either because they are humans equating themselves negatively with dogs, so whether it meant canines or temple prostitutes is not clear, though most scholars use the canine translation.

Kings, Job, and Hosea

The only other places the terms *qadesh* and *qadeshah* appear in the Bible are in the books of Kings, Job, and Hosea.

The passage in 1 Kings 14:23-24 is among the best with regards to making the religious aspects of this "prostitution" clear:

> "For they [Judah] also built for themselves high places (במות, *bamot*, as in either "hills" or "altars"), pillars (מצבות, *matsebot*, "pillars" or "sacred stones," including those dedicated to YAHWEH), and sacred poles (אשרים, *asherim*, the sacred poles named after and used in the worship of the Semitic pagan mother goddess Ahserah, which are always condemned in the Bible) on every high hill and under every green tree; there were also male temple prostitutes (קדשים, *qadeshim*) in the land. They committed all the abominations (תועבת. *to`ebot*) of the nations that the LORD drove out before the people of Israel." [NRSV].

The Septuagint's translation of this use of *qadesh* as "*syndesmos,*" which means "bond" or "ligament" does not seem to make sense. Some commentators have taken it as a reference to "sexual bonds," but that is not at all obvious. The translators of the Septuagint, knowing the Greek language of the centuries just before Christ, clearly were aware of both *porne* and the various words for homosexual partners, yet chose to use neither of them. Some 500 years later, Jerome's use of *effeminati* in his translation into the Latin Vulgate is both inaccurate and unfortunate.[32] There is no reason to assume that the temple prostitutes were "effeminate," and even if they had been, no reason to associate a specific pagan practice with effeminate men in general. The two most common early English Bibles – the Catholic Douay Bible and the Protestant/Anglican King James Bible – both have equally inaccurate translations. Douay simply mimics the Vulgate. The King James Bible uses the word "sodomite," which is problematic on two accounts. As we've already discussed, there is no clear evidence that the

---

[32] St. Jerome, Eusebius Sophronius Hieronymus (c. AD 347-420), who translated the Bible from Hebrew and Greek into Latin, giving the Church the Vulgate, was known to be a severe ascetic with generically dim views of sexuality and a staunch defender of clerical celibacy (at that time not yet a common mandate) and the perpetual virginity of Mary (a theological assertion about Mary's life not to be confused with the virgin birth of Jesus Christ). Given those views, it is easy to see why he did not bother to distinguish between the cultic and commercial versions prostitution. Sadly, the sex-negative attitudes of this one man have permeated all of Western culture (and from there spread to the East as well) because the Vulgate, rather than the original Greek and Hebrew, became the source of later vernacular translations of Scripture, and many of the Renaissance and Reformation translators, steeped themselves in the sexual morality that had evolved in this milieu, either did not realize or did not care to explore the nuances of the original languages' words for such sexually oriented acts.

"sin of Sodom" was sexual. Furthermore, the sin of the *qadeshim* was not their sexual activity, but their idolatry.

Many fundamentalists, while arguing against modern scholarship regarding homosexuality and the Bible, insist that the *qadeshim* were cult prostitutes who engaged in sex with other men. These authors claim, without much evidence, that the so-called "revisionists" (the scholars who accurately translate the Bible with regards to homosexuality) claim that the *qadeshim* were heterosexual cult prostitutes who engaged in sex with female clients. Both arguments miss the point entirely. It is irrelevant whether the *qadeshim* engaged in sex with men, women, or both. The source of their immorality is not sexual, but cultic. They are not immoral for having homosexual or heterosexual sex. They are not immoral because there may have been an exchange of money. They are immoral because visiting them was a means to worship a pagan god. As always, the chief moral concern of the Bible is idolatry.

The term *qadesh* is used three other times in the books of Kings – 1 Kings 15:12, 1 Kg 22:46, and 2 Kg 23:7. Unlike when translating the Pentateuch, the Septuagint never uses *pornos* as a translation of the Kings verses. In fact, it uses four entirely different words. *Syndesmos* as discussed above in 1 Kg 14:24, *teletas*[33] in 15:12, and *endiēllagmenou*[34] in 22:46. Neither of these words means "prostitute" and neither is a reference to homosexuality. In 2 Kings 23:7 the Septuagint simply writes the Hebrew word in the Greek alphabet, καδησιμ without translating it at all. It is impossible to say whether the translators of the Septuagint were confused by the term, understood it and wanted to avoid it, tried in ways that are no longer clear to explain it, or some combination thereof.

---

[33] This Greek translation is also obscure, as *teleo* generally relates to being fulfilled or complete, though it also has uses related to taxation and, perhaps most relevant here, to be initiated in the rites of Bacchus.

[34] Much to-do is made about this Greek word, a participle of αλασσω *allassō*, "change," meaning roughly "one who has changed." Some anti-gay commentators try to make it refer to transvestism or "becoming like a woman" while others point out that it could refer to changing one's religion from Judaism to paganism. Perhaps the Septuagint translators were closer to the context and understood details about the *qadeshim*; on the other hand, it is equally (or even more) likely that they had little understanding of religious practices hundreds of years prior to their work and used a word they felt appropriate based upon the practices of their time and place. Nonetheless, it is at least odd that the Septuagint uses several entirely different words to translate the Hebrew into Greek, which seems to indicate a lack of understanding of the term's true meaning. In any case, the original meaning is not dependent upon the accuracy or inaccuracy of a translation, even a very ancient and revered one.

Unfortunately Jerome was consistent in his Vulgate, translating all four of the Kings passages as some form of "effeminate." This carried over to the English Douay Bible. The King James Version repeated its error from Genesis 38 translating the term as "sodomites," which is also found in some Spanish Bibles. Most modern English translations have used something similar to "cult prostitute," and some have even given more elaborate explanations such as *Good News for Modern Man's* "men and women who served as prostitutes at those pagan places of worship." A small number of modern translations have inconsistencies between these verses, such as the *New American Standard Bible's* "sodomites" in 1 Kg 22:46 while using "male cult prostitutes" in the other Kings passages. The *Biblia Latinoamerica*, a very common Spanish Bible in Latin America, uses "*homosexuales sagrados*" ("sacred homosexuals") in two places and "*prostitutos*" in the other two places. Sadly this leaves the burden on gays and commercial prostitutes when in fact the verses are clearly discussing pagan religious practices, not homosexuality or modern prostitution.

The Job passage is not discussing prostitution at all, but uses the *qadeshim* as a reference. It is saying that the godless die young, like the *qadeshim*. Whether or not the sex-priests were commonly short-lived, or whether this was an assumption or an ancient stereotype, is not clear, but it is at best tangential to the point, since they are merely presented as an example. The Septuagint uses *titrōskomenē*, "wounded," and the Vulgate uses its infamous *effeminatos*. Modern English and Spanish translations use a variety of words, a few using a direct translation, others using different examples, perhaps after King James's "unclean," and a few simply avoid a translation altogether, simply saying "they die young." It is in this verse that the scholarly Spanish *Nuevo Biblia de Jerusalén* first uses the fascinating term *hieródulo*, which is not at all a common term in Spanish, but rather a transliteration of Greek *hieros doulos*, "priest slave." What is so fascinating about this Greek transliteration is that it is not from the Septuagint, though the Septuagint clearly set an ancient precedent when it transliterated קדשים as καδησιμ.

The Hosea 4:9-12 passage is another one where we get to see various words related to *zonah* and *qadeshah* in counterpoint. Here is my translation, in which I have left many of the uneasily translated Hebrew words untranslated.

> I will punish them for their ways and repay them for their deeds. They shall eat but
> not be satisfied; they shall have sex (*hiznu*) but not multiply because they have ceased to

hear YAHWEH. *Zənut,* wine, and new wine take their heart. The seek advice from their block of wood, and their stick tells them what they should do. A spirit of *zenunim* has led them astray, and they *vaiyiznu* from under their God. They sacrifice on the tops of mountains and burn incense on the hills, under oak, poplar, and terebinth, because their shade is good. Therefore your daughters *tizneynah* and your brides *tina'afnah.* I will not punish your daughters when they *tizneynah* or your brides when they *tina'afnah* for they go with *zonowt* and sacrifice with *qadeshot.*

The first occurrences are the verb *hiznu* and the noun *zənut* describing an activity. Both are related to *zonah.* The Septuagint translates them as *eporneusan* and *porneian,* respectively, both related to *pornē.* The Vulgate uses *fornicati sunt* and *fornicatio,* which are better described as transliterations of the Greek rather than true translations.

The next verse has the curious phrase *ruax zenunim,* which is translated as *pneumati porneias* and *spiritus fornicationum* in the Septuagint and Vulgate. The Hebrew, Greek, and Latin all use the same word associated with the Holy Spirit – *ruax, pneuma, spiritus.* Most modern language translations do the same, though a few use other words such as "urge."

Following this are past and future tense verbs, *vaiyiznu* and *tizneynah,* both related to *zonah.* They are translated *ekseporneusan* and *ekporneusousin (*based on *pornē)* in the Septuagint and *fornicati sunt* and *fonicabuntur* in the Vulgate.

For all of these occurrences some English translations reference "prostitution" or "whoredom" while others reference "fornication." *Today's English Version* likely gives the most accurate translations with such phrases as "You will worship the fertility gods" and "They have given themselves to other gods." However, in the midst of this carefully descriptive translation, the *TEV* also makes occasional reference to prostitutes, which is unfortunate. *The Message* paraphrases *vaiyiznu* with "they have replaced their God with their genitals." Once again this is a colorful image that tends to point the reader in the right direction – toward idolatry – and we wish that *The Message* had been more consistent in such innovation in other passages.

Most of the Spanish translations use versions of either *prostituir* or *fornicar.* The *Biblia Latinoamerica* provides clarity when it translates the past tense *vaiyiznu* as *"lo arrasta a engañar a su Dios con otros dioses."* However, this clarity is sadly damaged in the very next verse when it translates the future tense *tizneynah* as *"se hacen prostitutas."*

Next we come to the verb *tina'afnah* which is translated as *moixeusousin* in the Septuagint and *adulterae erunt* in the Vulgate. Almost all modern translations use some form of "adultery" for the translation. Like with "prostitution," there has been little effort to correct assumptions as to what "adultery" means in the biblical context.

Finally we come across two more nouns, *zonowt* and *qadeshowt*, the feminine plurals of *zonah* and *qadeshah*. The Septuagint uses *pornōn* and *tetelesmenōn* while the Vulgate uses *meretricibus* and *effeminatis*, thus again inaccurately making reference to sex workers and effeminate men. As in 1 Kings 15:12, the Septuagint's use of a form of *teleo* is probably in conjunction with this verb's association with initiation into the rites of Bacchus. The Vulgate's use of *effeminatis* to translate what is already a reference to a female sex-priestess is odd.

Most English translations add to the confusion by using "harlots" or "whores" for the feminine *zonowt* and "temple prostitutes" or some synonym thereof for the *qadeshowt*. *Today's English Version* says, "You yourselves go off with temple prostitutes and together with them you offer pagan sacrficies," conflating both terms into the same idolatrous action, making this the best of the published English translations.

Most of the Spanish translations do similar things. The *zonowt* are called *prostitutas* or *rameras*, while the *qadeshowt* are given modifiers to clarify their cultic association, such as *"mujeres que practican la prostitución como un culto"* in *Dios Habla Hoy*. The *Antigua Versión* simply calls them *malas mujeres* ("bad women"), sadly reinforcing the stereotype that being "bad" is presumably something sexual, especially when a woman is involved.

Once again we have a detailed account of these activities that betrays the concept that there is a clear-cut distinction between *zonah* and *qadesh*, thus weakening the argument that the Bible condemns modern (non-religious) sex workers because they are *zonowt* while the temple sex-priests were *qadeshim*.

"Prostitute" in the Book of Kings

Hebrew	Septuagint	Vulgate	English	Spanish
1 Kings 14:24 קדש qadesh	συνδεσμος syndesmos (band, bond, joint tie, uniting principle)[35]	effeminati	effeminate [D] sodomites [KJV] male temple prostitutes [NRSV] male prostitutes [REB] cult prostitutes [NAB] male sacred prostitutes [NJB] men and women who served as prostitutes at those pagan places of worship [TEV] male shrine prostitutes [NIV] male cult prostitutes [NASB] male sacred prostitutes [Mes]	sodomitas [AVC] homosexuales sagrados [BL] consagrados a la prostitución [NBJ] los hombres practicaban la prostitución como un culto [DHH] se practicaba la sodomía [SBM] prostitución sagrada [BNP]
1 Kings 15:12 קדשים qadeshim	τελετας teletas	effeminatos	effeminate [D] sodomites [KJV] male temple prostitutes [NRSV] male prostitutes [REB] temple prostitutes [NAB] male sacred prostitutes [NJB] male and female prostitutes serving at the pagan places of worship [TEV] male shrine prostitutes [NIV] male cult prostitutes [NASB] sacred prostitutes [Mes]	sodomitas [AVC] prostitutos [BL] consagrados a la prostitución [NBJ] los hombres que practicaban la prostitución como un culto [DHH] sodomitas [SBM] prostitución sagrada [BNP]

---

[35] I cannot honestly figure out how *sundesmos* is a translation of *qadesh*. The Greek word appears four times in the New Testament, meaning either bonds (of peace or iniquity) or physical ligaments.

		"Prostitute" in the Book of Kings		
Hebrew	**Septuagint**	**Vulgate**	**English**	**Spanish**
1 Kings 22:46 קדש *qadesh*	ενδιηλλαγμενου *endiēllagmenou*	*effeminatorum*	effeminate [D] sodomites [KJV] male temple prostitutes [NRSV] male prostitutes [REB] cult prostitutes [NAB] male sacred prostitutes [NJB] male and female prostitutes serving at the pagan altars [TEV] male shrine prostitutes [NIV] sodomites [NASB] sacred prostitutes [Mes]	sodomitas [AVC] prostitutos [BL] consagrados a la prostitución [NBJ] prostitución sagrada [DHH] los que aún practicaban la prostitución como un culto [SBM] los sodomitas [BNP]
2 Kings 23:7 קדשים *qadeshim*	καδησιμ *kadēsim*[36]	*effeminatorum*	effeminate [D] sodomites [KJV] male temple prostitutes [NRSV] male prostitutes [REB] cult prostitutes [NAB] sacred male prostitutes [NJB] temple prostitutes [TEV] male shrine prostitutes [NIV] male cult prostitutes [NASB] male sacred prostitutes [Mes]	prostitución idolátrica [AVC] homosexuales sagrados [BL] consagrados a la prostitución [NBJ] la prostitución entre hombres que era practicaba como un culto [DHH] las meretrices sagradas [SBM] prostitución sagrada [BNP]

---

[36] This Greek is a transliteration, not a translation of the Hebrew, and adds further substance to the idea that the translators of the Septuagint had no real understanding of what the Hebrew word meant.

"Prostitute" in Job and Hosea

Hebrew	Septuagint	Vulgate	English	Spanish
Job 36:14 קדשים *qadeshim*	τιτρωσκομενη *titrōskomenē* "wounded"	*effeminatos*	effeminate [D] unclean [KJV] in shame [NRSV] male prostitutes [REB] the reprobate [NAB] male prostitutes of the temple [NJB] life of disgrace [TEV] male prostitutes of the shrines [NIV] cult prostitutes [NASB] living it up in sexual excesses [Mes]	sodomitas [AVC] despreciada [BL] hieródulos [NBJ] en forma vergonzosa [DHH] siendo despreciada [SBM] *(not really translated)* [BNP]
Hos 4:10 הזנו *hiznu*	επορνευσν *eporneusan*	*fornicati sunt*	they have committed fornication [D] they shall commit whoredom [KJV] they shall play the whore [NRSV] (they will) resort to prostitutes [REB] they shall play the harlot [NAB] they will play the whore [NJB] you will worship the fertility gods [TEV] they will engage in prostitution [NIV] they will play the harlot [NASB] (they will) have sex [Mes]	fornicarán [AVC] se prostituirán [BL] se prostituirán [NBJ] se prostituirán [DHH] se prostituirán [SBM] fornicarán [BNP]

"Prostitute" in Hosea				
Hebrew	Septuagint	Vulgate	English	Spanish
Hos 4:11 זנות zənut	πορνειαν porneian	*fornicatio*	fornication [D] whoredom [KJV] whoredom [NRSV] immorality [REB] harlotry [NAB] whoring [NJB] *(not included)* [TEV] prostitution [NIV] harlotry [NASB] rutting with whores [Mes]	fornicación [AVC] prostitución [BL] prostitución [NBJ] prostitución [DHH] la vida libertina [SBM] fornicación [BNP]
Hos 4:12 ראח זנונים ruax zənunim	πνευματι πορνειας pneumati porneias	*spiritus fornicationum*	spirit of fornication [D] spirit of whoredoms [KJV] spirit of whoredom [NRSV] spirit of promiscuity [REB] spirit of harlotry [NAB] urge to go whoring [NJB] like a woman who becomes a prostitute [TEV] spirit of prostitution [NIV] spirit of harlotry [NASB] drunk on sex [Mes]	espiritu de fornicaciones [AVC] espiritu de infidelidad [BL] espiritu de prostitución [NBJ] dominado por la prostitución [DHH] espiritu de libertinaje [SBM] espiritu de fornicación [BNP]

		"Prostitute" in Hosea		
Hebrew	**Septuagint**	**Vulgate**	**English**	**Spanish**
Hos 4:12 ויזנו *vaiyiznu*	εξεπορνευσαν *ekseporneusan*	*fornicati sunt*	they have committed fornication [D] they have gone a-whoring [KJV] they have played the whore [NRSV] they are unfaithful [REB] they commit harlotry [NAB] whoring they go [NJB] they have given themselves to other gods [TEV] they are unfaithful to their God [NIV] they have played the harlot [NASB] they have replaced their God with their genitals [Mes]	para fornicar [AVC] lo arrasta a engañar a su Dios con otros dioses [BL] se prostituyen [NBJ] se prostituye [DHH] hacerse libertinos [SBM] se prostituyen [BNP]
Hos 4:13&14 תזנינה *tizneynah*	εκπορνευσουσιν *ekporneusousin*	*fornicabuntur*	shall commit fornication [D] shall commit whoredom [KJV] play the whore [NRSV] turn to prostitutes [REB] play the harlot [NAB] play the whore [NJB] serve as prostitutes [TEV] turn to prostitution [NIV] play the harlot [NASB] are whores [Mes]	fornicarán [AVC] se hacen prostitutas [BL] se prostituyen [NBJ] se han prostutuido [DHH] se portan mal [SBM] se prostituyen [BNP]

		"Prostitute" in Hosea		
Hebrew	**Septuagint**	**Vulgate**	**English**	**Spanish**
Hos 4:13&14 תנאפנה *tina'afnah*	μοιχευσουσιν *moixeusousin*	*adulterae erunt*	be adulteresses [D] shall commit adultery [KJV] commit adultery [NRSV] commit adultery [REB] are adulteresses [NAB] commit adultery [NJB] commit adultery [TEV] commit adultery [NIV] commit adultery [NASB] are sleeping around [Mes]	adulterarán [AVC] engañan a sus maridos [BL cometen adulterio [NBJ] cometen adulterio [DHH] son adúlteras [SBM] adulteran [BNP]
Hos 4:14 זנות *zonowt*	πορνων *pornōn*	*meretricibus*	harlots [D] whores [KJV] whores [NRSV] whores [REB] harlots [NAB] whores [NJB] temple prostitutes [TEV] harlots [NIV] harlots [NASB] whores [Mes]	rameras [AVC] prostitutas [BL] prostitutas [NBJ] prostitutas [DHH] prostitutas [SBM] prostitutas [BNP]

<table>
<tr><td colspan="5" align="center">**"Prostitute" in Hosea**</td></tr>
<tr><td>**Hebrew**</td><td>**Septuagint**</td><td>**Vulgate**</td><td>**English**</td><td>**Spanish**</td></tr>
<tr>
<td>Hos 4:14
קדשות
qadeshowt</td>
<td>τετελεσμενων
tetelesmenōn</td>
<td>*effeminatis*</td>
<td>effeminate [D]
harlots [KJV]
temple prostitutes [NRSV]
temple-prostitutes [REB]
prostitutes [NAB]
sacred prostitutes [NJB]
(offer pagan sacrifices) [TEV]
temple prostitutes [NIV]
temple prostitutes [NASB]
worship at the holy whorehouses [Mes]</td>
<td>malas mujeres [AVC]
consagrados a la prostitución [BL]
consagradas a la prostitución [NJB]
mujeres que practican la prostitución como un culto [DHH]
prostituas de culto [SBM]
rameras del templo [BNP]</td>
</tr>
</table>

Just What Is a *Zonah*?

This is an important but difficult question. As we have seen, the word is usually translated at "prostitute," "harlot," "whore" or something similar. Some commentators and translators have attempted to make a clear-cut distinction between a *zonah* and a *qadeshah*, calling the *zonah* a "common" prostitute (or some variation thereof) and the *qadeshah* the cultic or "temple" prostitute. However, this distinction is not clear in the Bible and it further creates the image of modern-day sex workers being discussed in the Bible along with, but separate from, the sex-priests and sex-priestesses.

So just as we explored what the *qadeshim* and *qadeshot* were, we must do the same with the *zonot* (feminine plural or *zonah*). The word usually means "prostitute" in modern Hebrew, and *ben-zonah* ("son of a *zonah*") is the slang Hebrew equivalent to "son of a bitch" in English.

The etymology of the word is not absolutely certain, but it probably is related to the verb זון zown, "to feed." Through the ages there has been much discussion concerning Rahab, the zonah mentioned in Joshua 2:1. Rahab was the great-great-grandmother of King David, and thus an ancestor of Jesus. (See Matthew 1:5). Some rabbis have argued that Rahab was not a zonah/prostitute, but rather a zunah/hostess. (This is only the difference of one vowel, and that being the position of the dot above or within the ו [w], and the Bible was originally written without vowels, so both would appear ZWNH.) While this historic discussion may have initiated as a result of anti-prostitution attitudes and the desire to not have either David or Jesus descended from a prostitute, it does raise many doubts as to exactly what the word meant three thousand years ago.

The Septuagint calls Rahab a γυναικος πονης (gunaikos pornēs, "woman prostitute") in Joshua 2:1, and the New Testament picks this description up as well (Hebrews 11:21 and James 2:25). This cannot, however, be taken to mean with certainty that the word originally meant "prostitute," but only that by the third century B.C. it had come to mean so.

The relationship between zonah and zunah is extremely interesting. One possible etymology is that the word originally meant well-fed and this evolved into "wanton" which further evolved into connotations of prostitution. Even in English it does not take too great an imagination to conjure up graphic images as to how a prostitute might be described as "well-fed."

We should also note that, once the modern viewpoint of severe sex-negativity is put aside, the difference between a "hostess" and "prostitute" may not be so great. Envision oneself three thousand years ago in the desert, long before Las Vegas and Hollywood, before hotels and motels, but also long before the brothels of ancient Rome. Imagine a woman running an inn out of her tent. She feeds her guests and provides them shelter from the harsh world outside. Maybe she lets them sleep in her bed. Maybe she provides sexual favors to most of her guests, maybe to only some, and maybe never. Maybe she charges more if they sleep with her, maybe not. Maybe some of her guests also aren't hungry and she doesn't feed them either. Maybe they get a discount if they don't eat, and maybe they don't. Now the modern eye's sharp distinction between zonah and zunah has disappeared, no longer clouded by our obsession with sex.

There are several potential Arabic cognates, including *zanaya*, "to have illicit sex." However, one must be very careful when comparing cognates in modern or even medieval languages, because the word's new meaning could have evolved based upon false but common assumptions about ancient meanings (as with "fornication," the English cognate of *pornē)*. There is also *zanâ*, "to provide refuge or lodging," akin to the "hostess" meaning of ZNWH. A *zanûn* is someone untrustworthy. Most interesting, however, is *zûn*, an idol or any deity other than God. This hints at a possible ancient connection between the *zonah* and idolatry, just as we found with the *qadesh*.

In modern religiously strict Judaism the issue of the word's meaning comes up because Leviticus 21:7 prohibits a priest (*kohen*) from marrying a *zonah*. It is very interesting that medieval and early modern rabbis did not think this meant that the priest simply cannot marry a prostitute (or a divorced woman or a non-Jew, the other two groups prohibited in addition to a *zonah*). It is further interesting that their definition of the term had specifically *religious* qualifications – that it was a regulation about the purity of the nation, not so much about sexual activity.

Rabbi Moses Maimonides (AD 1145-1204), in the *Issurei Biah* section of his *Mishneh Torah*, dealt specifically and directly with the meaning of the word:

> From a tradition we have learned that the Zonah described in the Torah is any woman who is not a Jew [lit. "daughter of a Jew"], or a Jew who had sexual relations with a man to whom she was prohibited to marry [Nissuin] by a prohibition which applies to all, or if she had sexual relations with a Challal [progeny of a Kohein and a woman who is forbidden to him] even though she is permitted to marry him. (*Issurei Biah* 18:1)

The *Shulchan Aruch*, the most authoritative legal code of Judaism, authored by Yosef Karo in AD 1563 and published in Venice, describes very specific cases of when a woman is or is not a *zonah*. (*Even HaEzer* 6:8):

- A convert or a freed Canaanite maidservant are *Zonot* in all cases because they did not start out Jewish.

- A woman who had relations with an animal is not a *Zonah* because she didn't have relations with a man to whom she was prohibited to marry.

- A woman who had relations while being a *Niddah* or as a prostitute (to an otherwise kosher man is **not** a *Zonah* because the man having relations with her can still marry her. [Emphasis mine.]

- A woman who is a widow and had relations with a Kohein Gadol ["high priest"] does not become a Zonah because that prohibition (Kohein Gadol to widow) is not one that applies to all.

Again we note that, as with Maimonides, the issues of concern are primarily religious, not sexual. The most interesting, of course, is the specific declaration that a prostitute is not a *zonah* if her client is Jewish. Presumably this would mean all of her clients, because the basic issue is that the woman is not to bring the uncleanness of a non-Jew to the *kohen*.

As with the exact nature of the *qadesh*, the exact nature of the *zonah* of 1,000 BC may be lost in antiquity. It does, however, shed serious doubt on the argument that the Bible categorically condemns prostitution.

Other Occurrences of *Zonah*

Throughout the Old Testament the verb *zanah* is used 66 times. The noun *zonah* is used 33 times, and *zənunim* is used 12 times. The abstract noun *zənut* is used 9 times. In approximately half of these occurrences there are clear religious connotations, with phrases that are translated in manners such as "prostituted themselves by following other gods." In other cases the usage is more general and refers to "unfaithfulness" and is even sometimes translated "adultery," though not necessarily in a sexual sense. In some passages the term is simply used to describe someone in a story, though whether or not they were prostitutes of any sort is not pertinent to the story itself. In such cases it could just as accurately be translated "person." It is only a minority of the uses of any of these *ZNH* words that sex for pay is distinctly implied. These also tend to be later in the Old Testament, indicating that perhaps the word's exact meaning evolved during the course the nearly two millennia represented by the Old Testament.

So Now What Is a *Pornē*?

The New Testament occasionally uses the words πορνη (*pornē,* a concrete feminine noun) and πορνος (*pornos,* a concrete masculine noun), and, as we have seen, the Septuagint sometimes uses these words in its translation of the Hebrew Bible. The abstract noun πορνεια (*porneia*), and the verb πορνευω (*porneuō*) are used as well. Although the concrete nouns are often relatively accurately translated as "prostitute" or some synonym thereof, the abstract noun and the verb forms many times lose any reference to prostitution. This follows Jerome's frequent transliteration of the words into Latin as *fornicatio* and *fornicare*. It is vital to note that these are not real translations, but rather transliterations that merely take a Greek word and put it into Latin. It is much the same as the Septuagint's use of καδησιμ for קדשים in 2 Kings 23:7. It is a way to avoid assigning any real meaning to the foreign language's term.

Unfortunately this transliteration has taken root in many modern languages, such as "fornication" in English and *fornicación* in Spanish, both usually meaning some generic form of "illicit" or "inappropriate" sex, including premarital or extramarital sex of either heterosexual or homosexual nature. But this is clearly *not* what the original Greek word meant.

One must be careful of improper translations and discussions of the Greek. Many of the "old" dictionaries of Biblical Greek were compiled in the Victorian era and made no real effort to discuss the real meaning of *pornos* and its related words. Some of them discuss the relationship between the nouns and the verb *porneuō,* implying that this much later concept of "fornication" is an underlying concept in ancient Greek language. They fail to point out the true etymology of the words, being derived from περνημι (*pernēmi*), which means "to be sold." *Pernēmi* is a passive form of the verb *peraō* which basically refers to taking something across the sea to sell it. Understanding this gives a much clearer understanding of the *pornē* and *pornos*. Originally they were slaves, women and men, brought from overseas and sold (or more technically rented out) for sexual favors. In today's world they would be considered the victims of human trafficking.

The Latin words *prostituta* and *prostituto* are reasonable translations of the original meaning of *pornē* and *pornos*. This is true not only denotatively, but also connotatively, and even in a curious way etymologically. *Prostituta* derives from *pro-statuere*, literally "to stand up front." This is because the *prostitutae* were forced to stand out in front of the brothels by their owners so that clients could choose them.[37] Thus they were *pernēmi,* "sold," by *prostatuendi,* "standing out front."

Commercial prostitution was common in ancient Greece. In spite of the openness of Greek society to bisexuality, where it was the norm, at least for upper-class men, to have both male lovers and wives, there were certain sexual acts that were considered "improper" for a citizen, and these were often provided by male and/or female slave-prostitutes. These were the *pornoi* and *pornai,* who were at the bottom of the scale of types of sex workers.

The owners of the *pornoi* or *pornai* were the πορνοβοσκοι (*pornoboskoi,* essentially "pimps"). Similar to modern pimps, they kept a portion (or even all) of the wages of their slaves' earnings. In the earlier times of ancient Greece, they were all slaves brought from overseas (hence the etymology) but by the time of Plato children abandoned by their citizen parents could become *pornoi* or *pornai.* Being a *pornoboskos* was considered a legitimate but disreputable profession. In his book *Characters,* Theophrastus (371-287 BC) writes concerning the Απονοια ("Rough"), "He is the sort of man to keep a hostelry, or brothel, or to farm the taxes. There is no business he considers beneath him, but he is ready to follow the trade of the crier, cook, or gambler."[38] It is very curious, given our prior discussion of the Hebrew *zanah* and *zonah,* the innkeeper and the prostitute, that this Greek living several centuries later still considers innkeepers and pimps to be similar in character.

Not all of the *pornoi* and *pornai* were slaves. Independent prostitutes were registered and taxed in Athens, and some made considerable amounts of money. The *pornai* were among the only women actually allowed to handle money. They were not held in great repute in Greek culture, but this is mostly from being perceived as greedy rather than promiscuous. Their greed was a common theme of jokes, and there were many attempts to regulate the price of prostitution in ancient Greece. Part of this "greed," however, derived from the real-world

---

[37] Curiously, the word "prostitute," considered the more proper and acceptable term, is derived from this form of slavery while the word "whore" ultimately derives from the Proto-Indo-European root *kā* which is also the source of Latin *caritas* ("love" or "charity"), leading to French *cher* and Spanish *caro,* both terms of affection meaning "dear."

[38] *The Characters of Theophrastus,* translated by Charles Bennett and William Hammond, p. 51. (1902, New York: Longmans, Green, and Co.) Available online at http://archive.org.

need to accumulate wealth to last into one's later years, when one's services had been replaced by younger prostitutes.

It was rare for a citizen to be a *pornos*, and if a citizen was one, it carried political costs, including possible loss of public rights. There are legal accounts where the testimony of a person has been challenged on the basis of that person's allegedly being a *pornos*. The theory was that someone who sold his or her body could also sell his or her testimony or vote. Once again, the stigma is more related to the perception of greed than to any concept of promiscuity.

Ancient Greece also had another class of "prostitutes" termed ἑταιρα (*hetaira*), which literally means "companion" and is the feminine form of ἑταιρος (*hetairos*) used for the noblemen in Alexander the Great's army. Unlike the *pornai*, the *hetairai* were educated and provided more the just sexual favors.

Is a *Qadesh* a *Pornos*?

In the deuterocanonical book of 2 Maccabees, the author describes the desecration of the Jerusalem Temple by the Greek occupiers after Alexander's conquest. The Temple was rededicated to Zeus and "was filled with debauchery and reveling by the Gentiles, who dallied with prostitutes and had intercourse with women within the sacred precincts, and besides brought in things for sacrifice that were unfit." (2Mac 6:4, NRSV). The Septuagint uses μεθ ἑταιρων (*meth hetairōn*) for what is translated "with prostitutes." (And the "women" in the verse are simply *gynai*, the common term for "women.")

The Corinthian temple of Aphrodite also was known to have priests who performed sexual favors. Strabo, the Greek historian writing around the time of the Birth of Christ, commented about Corinth, "And the temple of Aphrodite was so rich that it owned more than a thousand temple slaves, courtesans, whom both men and women had dedicated to the goddess. And therefore it was also on account of these women that the city was crowded with people and grew rich; for instance, the ship captains freely squandered their money, and hence the proverb, 'Not for every man is the voyage to Corinth.'"[39] The Greek word translated "courtesans" is *hetairai*.

Given its own use of *hetaira* in Maccabees, it is intriguing that the Septuagint does not use this word to translate *qadesh* and *qadeshah* in the Pentateuch, but rather uses *pornos* and *pornē* (and uses a variety of strange terms in the rest of the Old Testament translation). The reasoning behind this difference may be lost in antiquity, but probably include the fact that the Septuagint had many different translators (hence its name, which means "seventy," the traditional number of its translators). It is safe to say, however, that the Septuagint, or perhaps others prior to it, set the way for the Greek word *pornos* and its derivatives to take on association with the sex priests of the Old Testament. Likewise, it is safe to say that St. Paul and other New Testament authors were aware of this association.

Pornos in the New Testament?

The New Testament uses the various "*porn*" words a total of 56 times: *pornos* 10, *pornē* 12, *porneia* 26, and *porneuō* 8. *Pornē* is usually translated reasonably accurately (at least according to its original Greek usage) as "prostitute," "whore," or "harlot." The abstract noun (*porneia*) and the verb (*porneuō*) are typically translated with the technically meaningless transliteration of "fornication" or "to fornicate" or sometimes even less accurately as "immorality," "impurity," or "sexual immorality." These loose and poor translations do a great disservice to Scripture by introducing a sex-negativity that is not in fact present. The masculine concrete noun (*pornos*) is often translated as "fornicator" or, as in the King James Version, "whoremongers," which term is particularly odd because it denotes the one who visits a prostitute rather than the prostitute himself.

In many cases it is not clear whether these words referred to cultic or commercial "prostitution." For example, Matthew 5:32 and 19:19 gives *porneia* as a justification for divorce. Does this mean that a man can divorce his wife if she served as a sex-priestess, or a lower-class slave-prostitute, or perhaps both? It is not entirely clear, but saying that

---

[39] Strabo, *Geography*, Book VIII, Chapter 6, Verse 20, available on the internet at
  http://penelope.uchicago.edu/Thayer/E/Roman/Texts/Strabo/8F*.html

"fornication" is a cause for divorce, in modern languages adds an entire spectrum of excuses not accurately covered by *porneia*. Either of the legitimate possible translations provides a better rationale for divorce – the idolatry associated with being a sex-priestess or the commercial independence and/or dependence upon another man (the "pimp") of commercial prostitution – both of which would contradict the "wife as the man's property" presumption of marriage in New Testament times.

Likewise many of the condemnations in the Epistles against being a *pornē* or *pornos* are not entirely clear whether they are talking about the sex-priests or the commercial prostitutes. The presumption that it refers to the cultic aspects – the *qadesh* aspect – is more in tune with the general focus of Scripture on idolatry. It is easy to understand that the authors would condemn many of the aspects of ancient prostitution, but the logical focus would be on the slavery aspect thereof, and one would therefor anticipate a greater condemnation of the *pornoboskoi* (slave-trading "pimps") than the *pornoi* themselves. Many times the words are included in lists of other types of sinners, and those lists often include idolaters and sometimes *andrapoidistais* ("slave-traders" or "kidnappers") or *harpages* ("plunderers," "rapists," or those who capture slaves), both of which probably could refer to those who forced others into prostitution.

Perhaps the most colorful is the symbolic imagery of the Book of Revelation. In Chapter 17 we read:

> "Come, I will show you the judgment of the *pornēs tēs megalēs* ("great whore") who is seated on many waters, with whom the kings of the earth *hēs ekporneusan* ("have committed harlotry"), and the inhabitants of the earth have become drunk on the wine of her *porneia*. ... I saw a woman sitting on a scarlet beast that was full of blasphemous names (*onomatōn blasphemias*) ... having a golden cup in her hand full of the abominations (*bdelugmatōn*) and unleanness (*akathartētos*) of her *porneia*. And on her forehead was written a name, a mystery (*mustērion*), Bablyon the Great, the mother of the *pornōn* and the abominations (*bdelugmatōn*) of the earth. And I saw that the woman was drunk with the blood of the saints and the blood of the witnesses (*marturōn*) of Jesus."

We know that Revelation is apocalyptic ("hidden") literature, with a hidden meaning, and we now know that the "Whore of Babylon" is a description of the Roman Empire at the time of infant Church, "drunk with the blood of the saints and the martyrs of Jesus." We also know that the description is not a diatribe against prostitution, but is using the vivid imagery to describe the Empire.

The entire book is filled with religious symbolism, and this chapter is particularly vivid. The words it uses clearly identify the religious context, and thus the image of Babylon the Great *Pornē* is best envisioned as "Babylon the Great Pagan Priest."

"Blasphemy" has roughly the same (somewhat elusive, but clearly religious) meaning in Greek as in English. *Bdelugma* means "detestable" and is derived ultimately from *bdeō*, "to stink." It is used three times in the Gospels, once when Jesus corrects the Pharisees in Luke 16:14 and in Matthew and Mark with reference to the "abomination of desecration" – the idol that the Romans would later set up in the Temple. It is also the word used in the Septuagint to discuss the various ritual impurities in Leviticus, such as non-kosher animals and forbidden sexual practices (particularly those associated with the pagan religions).

Akathartes means "not clean" and is also used in the Gospels to describe "unclean spirits." It is the word in the Septuagint that translates טמא (*tame*) which means "foul" or "unclean" in a religious sense. For example, Leviticus 7:22 speaks of בבהמה טמאה (*bibǝhemah teme'ah*) which the Septuagint translates as τετραποδων των ακαθαρτων (*tetrapodōn tōn akathartōn*), "unclean beasts."[40] As with *bdelugma*, the word *akathartes* had clearly religious implications and was associated with the Levitical cultic regulations. Thus it seems clear that the *pornē* of Babylon was seen as a *qadeshah*, a sex-priestess, not as a commercial prostitute. Her abomination and uncleanness derive from her idolatry, not her sexuality.

Idolatry Once Again

Whether or not Paul or Moses would approve of a modern prostitute is neither known nor relevant. However, we must remember that *porneia* is a type of <u>idolatry</u>. Even though our modern culture tends to ignore and dismiss idolatry (such as holding a football game in a

---

[40] Literally "unclean tetrapod" in Greek, but the Greek word had not yet acquired its strict taxonomic definition of a "land vertebrate" – *i.e.* an amphibian, reptile, bird, or mammal. *Bǝhemah* means "beast" or "cattle," and its plural, *behemoth*, took on the meaning of a very large beast, most likely a hippopotamus in particular, hence the use of the term borrowed into English meaning something very large.

state-built stadium on a Sunday morning when moral people ought to be worshiping the True God), the writers of the Bible – both Old and New Testaments – considered idolatry and all its various manifestations the most serious of sins.[41]

It is safe to say that most modern prostitutes do not view themselves as priests or priestesses. Likewise, it is safe to say that most persons buying their services are not viewing it as an act of religious worship.

We must also not confuse the issues of forced prostitution with those of people who choose to exchange sex for money (whether they be advertising on the internet, standing on a street corner, or going out with someone who buys them dinner and drinks). Bringing people into the country and forcing them to work as prostitutes through abuse or threats of deportation clearly violates Biblical morality, but so would forcing them to clean houses or work in fields or sweatshops. The issue is not the sex, but the abuse. Condemning prostitution in general because of this abuse would be like condemning all government because some politicians were corrupt and abusing the system.

One can conclude, therefore, that the Bible does not address the issue of modern prostitution offered by those who freely choose it.

There are moral issues involved with premarital sex, but the issue is not that the sex has any inherent evil component, but rather that premarital sex, like other forms of sex, can be and is used in irresponsible and unloving manners. The most serious concern is that of unwanted pregnancy (and hence, premarital heterosexual activity is far more likely to be immoral than similar homosexual activity).

All children are entitled to be born into a home where they will be loved and wanted. In many cases premarital heterosexual sex opens up the potential that this basic human right will be compromised. Once the unwanted pregnancy occurred, the moral violation has been made. The options are abortion (a far worse evil yet), adoption, or raising the child to the best of the parents' ability.

This is not to say that pregnancy should automatically be followed by marriage, but to point out that the father and mother both have an equal moral duty to provide for the care and

---

[41] Yes, I *would* argue that the Bible writers would be far more concerned about state-sponsored sports events on Sunday morning than they would about women selling sexual favors on the street!

nurture of the child. What has happened happened, and the duty of both parents is to *put the child before themselves*. This may or may not mean that the mother and father continue their relationship with one another, but they forevermore *do* share a responsibility to the child.

It is immoral for heterosexuals to participate in procreative (*i.e.*, vaginal) sex without taking due contraceptive precautions unless they are ready to dedicate themselves to raising the child that could be born. Note that this would apply to married people as well as unmarried. Note also that this is almost directly the opposite of the conclusion of the so-called "natural law" theory of the Roman Catholic Church that considers sex without the possibility (however remote) of procreation problematic!

Other Sexual Issues

Bisexuality

Like the modern concept of homosexuality or the gay lifestyle, bisexuality was not a concept in the cultures from which our religious heritage is derived. This is certainly not to say there were not bisexuals as we understand them (people who are truly erotically aroused by persons of either sex). Nor is to say that many people did not experience sexual activity with both men and women. It is just to say that the psychological categories into which we place people were not yet defined.

In fact, bisexuality was probably extremely common, and perhaps even the norm for males of these ancient times. The reason why the Bible makes no commentary or condemnation of Jonathan and David's relationship is because there is nothing unusual about it. It was accepted as both factual and normal, and I am sure that the writers of Samuel would be surprised today to learn that some people even denied the relationship existed.

Because our psychological categorization is different, the concept of bisexuality itself does not appear in Scripture. Most fundamentalists would lump it together with homosexuality, and we could actually do the same. The difference, of course, would be that we would come to opposite conclusions to those of the fundamentalists.

There is no reason to believe that bisexuality is immoral. More importantly, we can categorically state that bisexuals, like their gay and straight brothers and sisters, are fully entitled to the Love of God. Heaven is certainly populated with countless persons who lived on earth as bisexuals.

Some people (both gay and straight) argue that bisexuality is a fiction or at least hypothesize that bisexuals are confused. This is not true. There certainly are many intrinsically homosexual people who live heterosexual lives as means of denial, conformity, or even presumed "repair" or their "problem." There are also people who are so overwhelmed by our culture's pressure to be heterosexual that this pressure blends with intrinsic homosexuality and results in confusion.[42]

Just because these people live an outward lie that contradicts their intrinsic makeup and betrays their personal integrity does not make them true bisexuals. And we must be very careful that we do not conclude that all bisexuals are liars or dis-integrated just because so many examples of gays trying to live straight lives appear to meet some outward definition of bisexuality. There are people who are *truly* bisexual.[43] They are sexually aroused by and/or emotively attracted to persons of both their own sex and the opposite sex. In fact, the now-famous "Kinsey scale" suggests that there is a continuum from pure homosexual to pure heterosexual through a whole array of bisexuality.[44]

On a moral level, there are two areas in which bisexuals (either true or apparent) receive extra condemnation. The first is that bisexual activity is intrinsically nonmonogamous. The second is that bisexuality gives the appearance of being "unnatural," even to some of those who accept that some individuals may be homosexual by nature. There is an implicit moral value placed on decisiveness, and the people who have such values tend to view bisexuals (especially open and honest "true" bisexuals) as the epitome of indecision.

All of these moral arguments against bisexuality *per se* are rather easily countered. Neither monogamy nor decisiveness, after all, can honestly be classified as important "biblical moral values." The Old Testament is full of polygamy, even among many of the biblical heroes.

---

[42] And, in theory, there could be some intrinsically heterosexual people who tried to deny or cure their heterosexual feelings by living homosexually, but it is difficult to imagine such a situation occurring in our heterosexist culture.

[43] I believe very strongly that *all* humans, probably all mammals, and perhaps even all vertebrates are by nature bisexual at some level. The more open we are to observing mammalian and avian behavior, the more we are learning that older research put inappropriate moralistic values onto other species. A good example is the so-called "monogamous" species of birds, some of which share their lives with the same opposite-sex partner, but who are not necessarily sexually exclusive with that partner even during the course of their monogamy. And, perhaps even more interesting, we are learning more and more about dolphin behavior, including the fact that the overwhelming percentage of male dolphins form life-long sexual pairs with one another, but clearly being a part of such a gay cetacean couple does not preclude mating with females.

[44] A rating of "6" is exclusively homosexual, and a rating of "0" is exclusively heterosexual in this 7-point scale. See Chapter 21, "Homosexual Outlet" of *Sexual Behavior in the Human Male* by Alfred Kinsey, Wardell Pomeroy, and Clyde Martin (Philadelphia: W.B. Saunders, 1948).

The Old Testament does not give a vision of sexual "fidelity" that is either self-consistent or consistent with modern society's views. (For that matter, the Bible's vision on the subject is inconsistent with what most people in modern society think the Bible says, whether those people agree or disagree with it.) While adultery is discussed, it was directly related to one male violating the property (female) of another male. The modern concept is more along the lines of a male violating the rights of his own wife by "cheating" with another woman (or another man). Thus a male's relationships with his other wives, concubines, or other males were not adultery in the Old Testament understanding because such acts were not violating another male's property.

One of the few benefits of the old system is that it essentially allowed bisexuality. Lesbianism was considered essentially irrelevant (and hence not condemned). Male homosexuality was tolerable because men had freedom to do as they wished sexually so long as they did not violate property rights (which would not include another free male) or commit idolatry with the sex priests or priestesses (who were, in a sense, the property of the false gods).

It is true that Jesus condemned indecision as far as one's relationship with Him, but indecision itself is neither portrayed in the Bible as inherently wrong, nor is it so perceived by our society. There is no evidence that the indecision (if there is any) associated with changing from a male to female lover is any more or less moral than the indecision associated with switching one's college major from English to math or one's occupation from teacher to mother or from dating a blond after having dated a black-haired person. Indecisiveness, no matter how dysfunctional it may become, has never been directly associated with immorality, so we have no business using it to condemn bisexuality.

The monogamy issue certainly can raise issues of fidelity to vows and relationships, as well as issues of honesty. These issues, of course, are not bisexual *per se*, but also can and do come up among heterosexuals and homosexuals. How does one find fulfillment as a bisexual and remain loyal and honest to one's partners? There are several options. The most obvious is serial bisexuality – for any given period of time the bisexual is in either a homosexual or a heterosexual relationship, but not both at once.

Some people, in fact, would say this is the only way a bisexual can live a moral life. We disagree. This puts us in the trap of making sex an idol and equating sexual exclusivity with marital fidelity. (See the following section on that subject.) It is possible to live an honest, loving, and hence morally acceptable life while acting out both aspects of one's bisexuality. Obviously it requires an honest, up-front, and understanding relationship with one's primary mate (who could even be another bisexual).

Another possibility is a bisexual polygamous relationship. None of these possible lifestyles is easy, and the multiple-partner issues may make the relationships nearly impossible to maintain. They may also be great breeding grounds for jealousy, resentment, revenge, and other similar potentially immoral behaviors. They may be highly dysfunctional. My point simply is that if they are open, honest, loving, and nurturing, they are neither intrinsically immoral nor clearly unbiblical. One must assume that Jonathan and Bathsheba knew about each other and their respective places in David's life.

Transgender Issues

If there is any group of individuals even more maligned by society than bisexuals, it is the various types of "transgendered" persons.[45] Obviously homophobic heterosexuals are part of the problem. Yet homosexuals are often no better. Forgetting for the moment how painful prejudice can be, these gays rebel against their sexual fringe groups perceived as even more extreme.

Ironically, it is often the so-called "politically correct" who are the most guilty. Some "normal" gay men are offended by drag queens because they supposedly reinforce the homophobic equation of male homosexuality with effeminacy. There are lesbian groups who denounce female-to-male transsexuals as "betrayers of womanhood" and will not admit male-to-female transsexuals because they "aren't real women." The immorality of this hypocritical bigotry should be obvious without further comment.

---

[45] The term *transgendered* is becoming the accepted generic term to include the whole gamut of persons with self-gender issues (*i.e.*, how they perceive themselves as opposed to how they react sexually to other people). It includes such different people as the cross-dresser who enjoys being sexual while wearing clothing normally associated with the other sex all the way to the postoperative transsexual who has essentially changed sex at the physical level.

The moral issues which people use to oppose transgendered people primarily relate to the concept of "nature." Obviously transsexuals (*i.e.*, those persons who have surgery to genitally make them members of the opposite sex) were unknown in either the Old or New Testament. Although there were "eunuchs" – usually defined as castrated males, though one cannot categorically say that this term, or the words translated into it, applied only to such a narrow or specific definition.

There is a passage in Deuteronomy (22:5) that calls it *to`ebah* for men to wear women's clothes and women to wear men's clothes. We must, however, again remember the whole context of the Old Testament law and how *all* modern people ignore the majority of its demands. We must also realize that the cross-dressing prohibition, being called "ritual impurity," may very well have been related to the Canaanitic fertility cult. Perhaps (and we really can never know for sure) the *qadeshim* (male cult priest-prostitutes) wore clothes traditionally associated with women.

"It's not nice to fool Mother Nature" still comes to mind to many (most?) people when they think of transsexuals. "If you were born a man, that means God wanted you to be a man" is the basic argument.

On the surface, the argument seems sound. On the other hand, a little deeper examination will expose our society's favorite idol – sex. The argument assumes that God really cares about gender; that assumption is false. Our gender is no more important to God than our hair color. Our physical sex is something (usually) determined at the genetic level just like our natural hair color. There may be countless arguments against dyeing or bleaching one's hair -- aesthetics, practicality, financial responsibility, health, etc. – but very few if any of us would argue that it is intrinsically *immoral* to change one's hair color. Why, then, would we make that argument about changing one's sex? Idolization of sex is the only reason. Interestingly, therefore, those who morally oppose transsexual changes for the transgendered people who want them are themselves committing a form of idolatry, and idolatry is, by definition, the *most basic immorality*.

We should also point out that gender is not as black and white (or male and female) as we usually assume. There are a whole variety of hermaphrodites.[46] There are even babies born with indeterminate or ambiguous genitalia who are erroneously identified by their mothers/ obstetricians/midwives and who are raised as the "wrong" gender according to their genetic makeup.[47] Simply put, we cannot categorically and absolutely declare that God made each of us either male or female and never the twain shall be unclear. That absolute dichotomy is just not true – it is not an accurate perception of nature. *Most* of us are XX or XY at the chromosomal level, but a few people are XXY or XYY. *Most* have either a penis or vagina, but others are born with both and others have neither.

If it were true that *genetic* sex type was always clear, that *genital* sex type was always clear, and that the two always agreed, the "don't fool Mother Nature" argument might hold some validity (but I would still argue it did not). Given that Mother Nature has already fooled us, the argument against transsexualism falls totally flat.

Furthermore, we have not even addressed the aspect that is probably the most important to most transgendered persons – the psychological or emotional. "Do I *feel* like a woman?" "Do I *feel* like a man?" To most of us those have never been serious questions. That does not make them unimportant for those persons who have gender mismatches at the psychological level. Their psychological mismatch is no less valid than the physiological mismatch of the XY baby (*i.e.*, genetically male) born with a vagina. If psychologically transgendered people desire to go to the time, effort, expense, and turmoil of correcting this mismatch, they should have earned our respect, not our disdain.

It is also worth noting that psychological gender identity is a different issue than the homo-/bi-/hetero-sexual continuum. There are some male-to-female transsexuals who become lesbians and some who become straight women. Likewise there are some female-to-

---

[46] Essentially persons of unclear sex, the term coming from a combination of the names of Hermes, the Greek messenger of the gods (Mercury), and Aphrodite, the Greek goddess of love (Venus), because their offspring were supposedly such intersexed individuals. This myth in and of itself is an interesting notation, indicating that the ancient Greeks recognized the fluidity of sex and gender, and even figured it would permeate the pantheon of gods.

[47] See, for example, *Gay, Straight, and In Between* by John Money, MD, (Oxford, 1990) which details much of the variety of hermaphroditism and pseudohermaphroditism.

male transsexuals who become gay men and some who become straight men. Nothing within this spectrum is inherently right or wrong.

It becomes a matter of making the best of one's life. For some that will mean accepting things as they are even though, given an initial choice, they would have chosen the other gender. For others it will mean making the physical changes. For still others, the decision will be somewhere in between.

God can and does love us independently of our gender – genetic, genital, or psychological – and independently of whether these are in agreement with one other.

Fidelity, Monogamy, and Sexual Exclusivity

These three terms – "fidelity," "monogamy," and "sexual exclusivity" are commonly interchanged, yet they mean quite different things. (Actually, "sexual exclusivity" is not part of the colloquial idiom, even though, as we shall see, it is the only proper term for what most people mean when they use the other two words.)

"Fidelity" means being faithful to a person or ideal. When used while talking about a marriage, it means treating one's partner with respect and giving him or her priority in one's own life.

"Monogamy" literally means "one marriage" (μονος γαμος). It is the system in which a person has only one spouse at a time. Strictly speaking, a monogamous person could have several sexual partners, so long as only one of these partners was in a live-in, committed, long-term relationship that had legal standing.

"Sexual exclusivity" means that two (or more) persons have sex only with each other. Note that a polygamous relationship could be sexually exclusive, as would be the case of a man with two wives who had sex with each of his two wives, but no one else, or the case of a bisexual man who had both a husband and a wife and had sex with each of them, but no one else. Obviously any dyadic relationship, whether male-female, male-male, or female-female, is capable of being sexually exclusive.

Fidelity is what we promise in wedding vows. This may or may not result in sexual exclusivity, and "faithful" marriages may be either monogamous or polygamous. Our society frowns upon polygamy, and there are many reasons why it is often not the ideal system. (One of the most obvious is the divorce rate among monogamous marriages. If it is so hard to keep two people working together happily, think how much harder it must be with three or more!)

It is essential, however, that we realize that it is our *society*, not our *religion*, that insists upon monogamy. (Religious institutions may have laws and canons against polygamy, but this is still the ecclesiastical hierarchy speaking about social issues, not religious or theological issues speaking for themselves.) As we have discussed before, Jacob and Solomon were respected religious people, and according to the Bible both were certainly polygamists.

Our point is not to tout the benefits of polygamy, but only to put it into perspective as something that is social, not religious or even intrinsically moral. Whether a person has one, five, or no spouses has no bearing on whether that person will go to heaven, whether that person is a "good Christian," or even whether that person is living a morally upright life (which also has nothing to do with going to heaven).

When we promise to be faithful to our spouses, that means that we will love them and cherish them, honor them, and do things that make them happy. *If* having sex outside of the marriage is something that will hurt the spouse in a real way, then doing so is a sign of infidelity. However, this is not necessarily or categorically the case. Many married people, both heterosexual and homosexual, enjoy and have even grown from sexual experiences outside of their marriages. In such cases of mutual agreement, it would be wrong to call the extramarital sex "infidelity."

When this happens in a marriage it is often a touchy issue. In most cases, though, the problem is not the sex itself but rather that one or the other of the spouses has not really thought the issue through. A spouse must be very careful not to suddenly conclude that extramarital sex is either (a) a sign that the marriage is ending or (b) a sign that s/he is not loved by his/her partner. The *worst* conclusion is the attitude so common among married partners. "If my spouse ever had an affair, I'd leave." *That attitude itself is an act of infidelity.* If we are to be faithful, we must remember "In sickness and in health." Even if, or perhaps especially if, an extramarital affair emanates from a hurt or trouble in the marriage, our commitment to remain faithful *demands* that we uphold our spouse and help him/her move through it. To do otherwise meets all the valid definitions of "infidelity." Very few marriages truly fall apart because of sex. They are destroyed by jealousy, selfishness, dishonesty, and lack of commitment.

The Bible is full of condemnations of adultery. Again, however, we must remember two things: (1) women were essentially property in the biblical cultures, and (2) adultery was often – perhaps usually or even always – a symbol for idolatry. We have evolved to a place in society where women are, at least superficially, treated as equals of men. Elaborate laws about adultery derived from the concept of a wife being a husband's exclusive property are not relevant today. Furthermore, most of our religions today do not involve overt sexual acts as part of worship. The connections between sexuality and religion are therefore clouded as we read Scripture. For the writers of the Bible, the connection was quite clear: Having sex with other people was a good analogy for worshipping other gods. In today's world we miss that metaphor and focus on the wrong thing entirely – the sexual acts, rather than the false liturgical practices they represent. If we were to really follow the message of the prophets, we would be far more concerned about doing good liturgy and keeping our inward hearts consistent with our outward worship than about such trivia as who sleeps with whom.

As Christians, too, we must be careful not to be led by either an overly literal interpretation of the Bible or by irrational emotions and the sex-negative upbringing so common in our culture. We are often called upon to help others with their problems (but never to judge them). Sometimes, although not always, extramarital affairs are signs of problems in a marriage, and we may be in a place to help the partners investigate and resolve these problems. Harping on the sexual issue would most likely be missing the point. We should help the partners communicate and resolve the negative issues that preceded the extramarital sex as well as those that arose with or because of it.

Likewise, we will most certainly encounter people who have developed a full, strong, and committed marital relationship that includes external sexual activity. This, for them, may be the most healthy and most beautiful expression of their sexual lives together. If it is working for them, it is not our place to interfere, condemn, criticize, or judge.

Certainly, though, we should not ignore the powerful emotion of lust and how it can be intertwined and confused with love. Separating the two emotions when dealing with extramarital affairs is important.

Lust itself is seldom the problem. A marriage can survive an honest and open encounter with extramarital lust. Such affairs will probably be short-lived. In order to remain faithful to one's spouse, the spouse in the lust relationship must (a) keep it in its proper place, that is, subordinate to the marriage and the spouse, (b) keep it from developing into a love that would threaten the marriage, and (c) keep it open and honest.

Honesty is such a vital moral concept that one should point out that there is a moral demand for honesty even in the lust relationship. Clearly it is immoral to let the lust relationship distract or damage the committed marriage (remembering that it is not the sex itself that does this damage). But it is also immoral to be dishonest to the lust-partner. Saying to one's lust-partner "I plan to leave my wife and be with you" when in fact a person has no intention of doing so is being dishonest and immoral in the lust relationship. Even subordinate relationships, whatever they be, demand our integrity, our openness, and our honesty.

In return for the openness and honesty in a marriage, the other spouse must not use the affair as an excuse to give up on or get out of the marriage (and thereby be unfaithful). The spouse involved in the lust affair must also be open and honest with the lust partner, and the spouse must be willing to terminate the affair if it begins threatening the marriage since the marriage-partner, not the lust-partner, has "priority in one's life."

In all cases, we must always come back to our basic point. *All people are loved by God.* We are saved by the merit of Jesus Christ, not our own. Our entrance to heaven has absolutely nothing to do with our sexual expressions or even with our marital loyalty.

To sum it up, "fidelity" and "monogamy" are intimately related. We have a moral responsibility to be faithful to our spouse (or, in a polygamous relationship, to our spouses). Basically one is unfaithful when s/he fails to give a spouse "priority in my life, second only to the LORD our God."[48] A relationship is, by definition, monogamous when there is *one* person with whom one has given such top-level priority.

The Sixth Commandment, "You shall not commit adultery," really means "You shall honor your commitments."

Divorce

We have just discussed how lust for another should not be allowed to destroy a marriage. However, there are marriages that are being destroyed by other factors, and sometimes a lust-affair becomes a symptom of that destruction. It is important to distinguish between symptoms and causes, but the distinction is not always clear. If one is in an otherwise stable marriage and begins to let that marriage fall apart because s/he is falling in love with someone else (regardless of whether s/he has had sex with the other love object), then the marriage is being polluted by adultery. Jesus alluded to this potential when He discussed adultery in the heart. It is not an extramarital sexual act that constitutes adultery, but the denigration of one's marriage in one's heart.

On the other hand, many marriages have fallen apart long before the affair ever began. The moral dynamics in such a case are quite different. Protection and honor of the marriage may be irrelevant. Protection and honor of the other spouse, though, are never irrelevant. One must be careful that s/he does not have an affair just for the purpose of vengeance against the other spouse. That is neither fair to one's (former) spouse or the affair-partner.

On the other hand, an extramarital affair can be a valuable experience in establishing one's self-confidence. This may be especially true when one is the victim of long-standing marital abuse. Obviously abusive marriages should be terminated. Divorce may involve breaking a vow, and that is not an honorable thing to do. However, there is an overriding and more important implicit vow to honor, respect, and protect oneself and one's children from an abusive person.

---

[48] From the marriage vows commonly used in the Ecumenical Catholic Church, *The Holy Eucharist and Other Sacramental Rites*, pages 297-298. (Riverside, CA: Healing Spirit Press, 1993)

Divorce in the case of an abused spouse is often the most moral choice available. It is a sign of one's mistake, but not of one's failure. We cannot mold other people into what they should be, and it is not our responsibility to teach our spouses to be nonabusive. It is our responsibility to protect ourselves.

Perhaps even more important is our responsibility to protect our children. Violence is a rampant evil in our society. It is never appropriate between two people, but is especially abhorrent when inflicted on a weaker victim by a stronger perpetrator. If children grow up in a violent atmosphere, they will most likely perpetuate this immorality. Parents have a moral obligation to remove their children from violence and abuse, even if that means destruction of a marriage.

In general, though, it is probably safe to assume that a two-parent family is a better situation for child-raising.[49] It is also true that divorce is traumatic for children. Couples with children, therefore, must take into consideration the well-being of their children when deciding whether to divorce. This does not mean that divorce cannot be the best moral choice for couples with children, but only that the children – and not solely the individual desires and benefits of the married couple – must be considered in the divorce evaluation process.

For example, a couple may decide that although they are content, they are not truly happy and they would both be better off ending their marriage and seeking new mates. After careful discussion and coming to true mutuality, divorcing could be a very positive thing for

---

[49] This generality, however, must be taken clearly within the context of its use herein, as it is a very limited and specific generality. One must carefully note that there are many, many situations, including some described in this work, where a single-parent family is clearly preferable to a dysfunctional dual-parent family. The reader must also note that there is absolutely nothing said about a male-female parenting situation and there is *no* justification for assuming that a heterosexual couple would be a better parenting team than a gay male or lesbian couple. Similarly, one must not construe this generalization to mean that specifically and purposely becoming a parent as a single person is wrong, immoral, or something that should not be done. If it were wrong to have children except in the most ideal of child-raising circumstances, then one would have to argue that most married heterosexual couples were not qualified either and that it is "immoral" for couples to have children if they are not of adequate financial means. It is incongruent to argue that only male-female couples should raise children because they are somehow "ideal" for the job (an assertion that we reject), and then not also argue that there should be at least some minimal financial, educational, genetic, and social criteria that a couple should attain before they could reproduce with moral integrity. It is intellectually dishonest to apply criteria in one arena and not in others, especially when some of the other criteria could be demonstrated even more factually than the alleged male-female superiority. (Which person, for example, if given a choice, would actually choose to be born to and raised by an uneducated, hateful man and an emotionally distant alcoholic woman, both living on the streets in abject poverty, rather than by surrogate parenthood to a loving and dedicated male movie star and his world-famous football quarterback husband who dedicate their lives to one another and to their child?)

them and the best moral option in their situation. If, however, the same couple had young children, the moral decision could be quite the opposite. Rather than focusing on their lack of perfect self-fulfillment, they might choose to concentrate on their contentment and remain committed to their children. They would have chosen to forego some personal satisfaction and advancement in order to protect their children from the trauma of divorce. (Note the distinction from the children's point of view between this situation, in which the divorce itself would seriously increase the overall family trauma, and the violent situation described above where a divorce would seriously reduce overall trauma.)

A special situation regarding divorce is the case of a homosexual person in a heterosexual marriage.[50] There are many social pressures that cause this situation. All of them are essentially dishonest. They cause people to lie to themselves, their spouses, and the world. There is nothing honest about living "in the closet," and honesty certainly is a paramount moral virtue.

Marriage is intrinsically (but not exclusively or even primarily) sexual. Therefore, there is an inherent flaw in the marriage of a homosexual[51] to a person of the opposite sex. Certainly the marriage can be a great partnership and can even be a spiritual union enhancing the pair's ability to minister on God's behalf.[52] It would be mistaken, however, to ignore the fact that some of the glue that holds the team together is missing in the heterosexual union of a homosexual person.

There is some argument that the heterosexual marriage of a homosexual person is entirely fraudulent. Some (or even most) probably are. There may be nonfraudulent cases when the marriage was entered into voluntarily, openly, and honestly by both partners, but these are probably rare. More likely, the gay or lesbian partner admits and/or discovers his/her homosexuality at some point in the marriage. The question of divorce or annulment

---

[50] Of course a heterosexual person in a homosexual marriage would be a moral parallel, but there is little if any social pressure for true heterosexuals to enter into gay marriages, so this parallel can essentially be ignored in the real world.

[51] As opposed to a true bisexual.

[52] As a sacrament, marriage is the union of baptized Christians through which God calls them to work and witness together as a team. It is akin to confirmation and ordination. The sexual, reproductive, and friendship aspects, while important, are not the reasons why Christian marriage is sacramental. There is no sacramental difference between gay or heterosexual marriage.

obviously arises. The canon law of the Ecumenical Catholic Church[53] recognizes the commonplace nature of this fraud and allows for annulment in those cases where the partners seek it. (Annulment is essentially a statement that some problem at the time of the wedding prevented the sacrament of marriage from taking place.) These canons do not consider the marriage of a homosexual with a heterosexual intrinsically *void*, but rather *voidable*. The difference is one of intent. Because the sacramental nature of marriage is not dependent upon its sexual component, and can exist even in the total absence of sexuality between the married partners, the gay-straight marriage can be valid if entered into openly and honestly. The ECC canons recognize that this is usually not the case – that the gay person who married an opposite-sex partner lied before, during, and/or after the marriage, and that this lie, this violation of integrity, is what prevented the sacrament from occurring, thus allowing the annulment to formally recognize this lack of sacramental union.

As in all divorce situations, the couple owe it to themselves, each other, their commitment, and their children (if any) to weigh the whole picture objectively and fairly. Just because something was initially based upon fraud does not mean it cannot through the course of time become real and uplifting.

There are some marriages, particularly mature, stable ones, which can and do weather this difficulty with flying colors. Both partners agree to stick it out because of their love, friendship, commitment, children, or any combination thereof. They may or may not allow for sexual exploration outside of the marriage. If they do so allow, they may or may not openly discuss it with each other. The trade-offs are complex. Allowing the partners to have extramarital sex will reduce some of the sexual tensions, but will increase the chance that they will fall in love in a way that significantly surpasses that of the marriage. The best arrangement will depend on the specifics of the relationship and the individuals involved. The moral imperative is to keep evaluating the progress and to be sensitive to the needs and growth of all involved.

Others find it necessary to terminate the heterosexual marriage as a part of the growth process. Although in most cases this probably turns out to be the best option, it should not

---

[53] Canon XX, Paragraph 10. *Canon Law, Articles of Incorporation, and Doctrinal Statements of the Ecumenical Catholic Church*, Revision 6.1. (Irvine, CA: Healing Spirit, 2001)

automatically be assumed or rushed into immediately upon the discovery or announcement of homosexuality.

When children are involved, parenting should be shared unless there is a true reason why one parent is not well fit. It is obviously incorrect to assume that the heterosexual parent will be the best parent.

Birth Control

The sexual functions of plants and animals evolved as a means of effecting evolution and facilitating variety within and between species. This fact, however, does not imply that procreation is the only legitimate reason for a person to have sex. If one were to accept that position, then one would also have to accept that the only legitimate reason to eat was to provide nourishment. Given acceptance of that position, there would be no room for exciting culinary adventures. From such a person we would expect sex only during fertile periods and through procreative mechanics. We would also expect that person to eat only those foods that provide the exact balance of nutrients needed, and then to eat them without unnecessary seasonings, preparations, or celebrations.

I hope this nutrition example sheds light on the preposterous notion that sex exists *only* for procreation. As human beings, we are entitled to enjoy the basic activities we have in common with other living organisms. Sex and eating are among the most significant. Being entitled to enjoyment means that sometimes we might change the activities slightly in such a way that does not further their animalistic purpose, but does enhance enjoyment.

Given this, it is an absurd, and even immoral, position to reject artificial birth control. We are living in a world where overpopulation continues to threaten our environment. There are even countries of the world where overpopulation threatens the very survival of individuals. To continue to have excessive children out of some sense of moral rectitude is, in fact, gross irresponsibility. For portions of the Church to continue to frown upon birth control is a serious error.

Curiously, the Roman Church has confounded the purity of its views on abortion because of its outdated views on birth control. If birth control were uniformly supported and encouraged, as well as freely available to all, there would be far fewer abortions. "Choice" and "life" are not opposite terms unless one takes away all opportunity for choice.

It is true that the proper time for choice is before, not after, conception. It is not fair, however, to enforce that position and then even eliminate the number of choices available before conception. As Christians we must always continue to support the tremendous value of all human life, but we must also facilitate the means by which life is created by choice, not by accident or ignorance. Thorough and complete sex education, together with freely available birth control, will facilitate this, and life is so much more important than trying to achieve perfect sexual propriety.[54]

AIDS and Disease

Disease is nothing new. There is evidence that dinosaurs suffered from cancer. We all know by our daily experience that not only people, but dogs, cats, birds, and even oak trees get diseases, and sometimes these disease kill.

In the last 100 years, we have learned a great deal about disease. Infectious agents of various sorts get into our bodies and cause problems. These agents can be transmitted from one body to the other by different means, depending on the infection involved. Although the mechanics and medical details can be quite complex, the basic concept is very simple. The mystery associated with disease has been wiped out by the knowledge gained through modern science.[55]

In most cases, disease is unpredictable and even sporadic. We know that certain events and activities can increase our chances of getting a disease, but there is still an unexplained random character. Smoking causes cancer, but not all smokers get cancer, and some people that have never smoked get cancer.

---

[54] The issue of abortion, and the morality or immorality thereof, is not a sexual issue, but one of respecting life. It therefore will not be discussed in depth in this work. Our personal belief is that abortion is evil and sinful, but the twisted ugliness of the so-called "pro-life" movement leads to serious doubt as to whether the government should legislate a moral position upon which there is such lack of uniform opinion. In this light, one might also distinguish between abortifacient birth control that occurs after fertilization and those methods such as condoms and birth control pills that prevent conception.

[55] Even though some diseases, including their specific causes, may remain mysteries, the generic mystery of disease, which pervaded all human thought until the discovery of causative agents, is gone.

There are a few diseases that are transmitted through sexual encounters. In the recent past, most of these diseases had been relegated to the category of "nuisance or embarrassment." People no longer go around worrying about dying of syphilis or gonorrhea, but in the not-too-distant past, however, these diseases were sometimes fatal.

Acquired immune deficiency syndrome (AIDS) is a relatively new disease in our species. Its origins are not fully understood, and a cure has yet to be found. Modern medical science has, however, done a remarkable job in finding the cause of this disease and discovering how it is transmitted. When blood or sexual fluids are taken from an infected body and absorbed into another, the virus enters a new host. This person may then become infected.

This is remarkably similar to how the common cold works. The differences are that a cold is easy to get and AIDS is very difficult to get. Because it can only be transmitted between people who share a relatively limited number of specific activities, it was originally confined to a few select populations. Gay males and intravenous drug users were the first groups infected in any large number.

Since many people frown upon both these groups of individuals, a few people set aside modern science and medical logic. They came up with preposterous positions, including the most repulsive of all, that AIDS was God's punishment for immorality.

Obviously these hate mongers did not understand the Bible. Long before science learned that disease had nothing to do with evil spirits or sin, Jesus knew this and explained it. The disciples asked Jesus whether a man born blind was born that way because he (the blind person) or his parents sinned. It was an either/or question, and the disciples assumed the blindness was a result of someone's sin. Jesus answered, "Neither he nor his parents sinned." (John 9:3)

No disease, including AIDS, is God's punishment for anything. That is not how God works. Furthermore, it is not even logical. At least two problems are raised by that false hypothesis.

If disease were caused by sin, we would have to conclude that the cold was God's punishment for the great and horrible sin of not washing one's hands, perhaps specifically for not following the Pharisaic regulations about washing. (We would also have to conclude that this sin of not washing hands was far worse than homosexuality because the cold is so much easier to catch than AIDS!)

We could justify our case for the common cold by looking into the Bible and citing God's moral demand for cleanliness. Leviticus, for example, is full of commandments to wash one's hands, clothing, and/or body after or before various happenings. We could even argue that Jesus promoted cleanliness and believed that washing in water cleansed from disease (John 9). Finally, we could even go so far as to point out that Baptism – the sacramental act through which we are reborn in Christ and become Christians – demonstrates the Church's universal commitment to the moral imperative to wash. Yet few, if any, believe that colds or other diseases that are known to be transmitted through poor hygiene are God's punishments for uncleanliness. We do not believe the common cold is God's retribution for failing to obey the moral commandments about washing. Why, then, can anyone logically conclude similar things about sexually transmitted diseases?

The second logical problem comes about when we try to explain how at least a few people get AIDS without committing the "sins" for which it is supposedly a punishment (such as a little child who had a blood transfusion).

Religious idiots have done a lot of damage when it comes to AIDS, and it is high time they stop. While the cure to AIDS itself lies in complex science, the cessation of its spread lies in simple education. When bigots and self-righteous "leaders" want to stop AIDS awareness, teaching children about prevention, and other sex education because it is "too graphic" or "might promote immorality," we who are true Christians must be ready to fight back with the facts that disease is not derived from sin, and saving lives is far more important than maintaining some sort of hypocritical moral code. Holding back information leads to suffering and death. Those who prevent awareness of AIDS are committing a sin that could even be classified as murder.

Most of all, we must assure every person with AIDS that s/he is still loved by God, and the disease is the result of a virus, not of "sin." Salvation, of course, has nothing to do with one's HIV status.

A Rational Sexual Morality

In spite of the strong statements regarding responsibility regarding sexuality, most importantly the responsibility to provide and care for any children born, some readers may think that we are advocating a total abandonment of sexual morality. Nothing actually could be farther from the truth. We do make two very strong arguments: (1) that salvation has nothing to do with morality, sexual or otherwise, and (2) that most of the moralistic statements made about sexuality are erroneous.

As should be apparent, however, we make some very strong statements about morality, and some of these apply either directly or indirectly to sexuality. The only real differences are that we disconnect morality from the essence of religion (salvation) because that is exactly what Jesus's Sacrifice meant, and also that our moral statements are approached from a rational standpoint over and above "traditional" interpretations (which often are not as traditional as their proponents choose to believe.)

In fact, some may find the moral statements already discussed and the ones following to be actually more difficult to practice than the more rigid but clear-cut positions promoted by fundamentalists. We contend, however, that the difference is akin to the relationship between the Christian Gospel and the Jewish Law. Certainly "Love you neighbor as yourself" is a far more difficult command than a whole series of "Thou shalt not's."

When we look at the Bible and the Old Testament law without the biases of modern prejudices and the sex-negative concepts we have been taught by our society, we find that the real issue in biblical morality was idolatry. So it should be today. We will see how sexuality remains idolatrous today and how we can avoid that idolatry, and thus be better servants of God. (Though again we must emphasize that following this path is not done to earn salvation or to avoid damnation, but rather because it is what most pleases God and what will ultimately lead to the best earthly life.)

The Family Idol

Perhaps the ugliest idol that we see today is the so-called "traditional family." This idol is widely worshiped in the conservative factions of most religions. It should be obvious to its worshipers that it is an idol when these people see agreement between groups who have traditionally held opposing theological viewpoints. There are Roman Catholics and die-hard Evangelicals who are joining together to worship this idol. Muslim and Christian fundamentalists alike bow at its feet, all the time pretending to be the true followers of their religion. While they cannot agree on the real tenets of their true religions, they find remarkable agreement in the false religion of "family values."

The reason that the family idol is so particularly heinous is because it cloaks its emptiness and poison under a gold-leaf facade of respectability, social responsibility, and "proper" religion. Like almost no other modern idol, this idol pretends to be True God, while it is in fact a golden calf. In order to distract its worshipers from the truth, it points to sexuality and calls "perversion" the golden calf.

This idol has established itself firmly on the altars of most churches. It is so clearly cemented in the Free Church denominations (Evangelicals, Baptists, Pentecostals, etc.) that whole campaigns are built around it. Holding the Scriptures in its hand, the family idol cloaks itself as the "word of God," leading its devotees to forget about the Incarnate Christ and His message of love. "Family values" replaces "Christ is risen" as the primary hymn of this religion.

In other circles the idol is less blatant and perhaps less well rooted. In the Anglican, Protestant, and Reformed churches, the idol prefers to set itself somewhat inconspicuously on the round tables of committees rather than on the central altar. While these groups often abhor the blatant bigotry of the "family values" charlatans, they nonetheless give the idol voice and vote on their committees and hold back truth and honesty in its name.

In the Vatican, we see the family idol starting to set itself on shelves in cardinals' offices and pontifical quarters. While Rome has normally been the domain of the fertility (procreation) idol described below, this idol has welcomed its more commonly worshiped sibling. The two sit side-by-side demanding respect from Roman Catholics and fostering the strange new friendship between the traditional theological foes in the Roman and Free Church camps.

The family idol spreads its immorality very insidiously among all segments of the population. Most obvious, of course, are the many Christians who have given up the Gospel Message to worship the family. Sadly, these former Christians may not even recognize their change in religion.

Yet the family idol does at least as much damage among those who would most vigorously reject it. That is because it falsifies itself as Christ Himself and, through this confusion, leads to the rejection of Christ. Confused by the lies of the worshipers of the family idol, many people who do not fit its narrow definition of "family" turn away from God and religion altogether. This, of course, is just another form of idolatry. The immorality of idolatry is not just worshiping the idol itself, but more importantly the lack of worship of the True God. It is strange that the churches that are so committed to evangelism on the surface have not recognized this destructive, anti-evangelical power of the family idol.

The symptoms of the family idol's worship are very strange. It equates a heterosexual, dual-parent, child-raising family with some sort of moral ideal. While there is rational and empirical evidence that children may be better off in a two-parent family, there is no evidence that a heterosexual pairing is any better than a homosexual pairing. Furthermore, there is remarkable evidence that single-parent families are successful in raising well-rounded, balanced children. Most (or even all) children are not raised in ideal surroundings, so there is no reason to hold the two-parent ideal as any more important than economic, intellectual, geographic, nationalist, or other "ideals." Empirical evidence indicates that white American children have more opportunities than those of other races, yet no one would suggest that only white families should reproduce. The same argument in favor of heterosexual families is equally invalid.

Yet the family idol and its devotees use ignorance to promote themselves. They make ridiculous statements such as one heard from Focus on the Family[56] that imply that the children of committed lesbian couples would have problems that were intrinsically related to

---

[56] A political group founded by James Dobson and headquartered in Colorado Springs, Colorado, devoted to the worship of the family idol. www.focusonthefamily.com

their mothers being a lesbian, rather than heterosexual, couple. Obviously the moral character, dedication, and quality of parents – not their sexual orientation – are what determine whether the child will grow up healthy, functional, and morally upright. Yet because of ignorance people fall for the propaganda of Focus on the Family, the Traditional Values Coalition,[57] the American Family Association,[58] the National Organization for Marriage,[59] and other groups that dedicate themselves to the idolatrous worship of their own definition of a "traditional family" and its so-called "family values."

These groups do great harm to the people who do not fit their narrow concepts. They also draw people away from God because they present a false image of God. They present a hateful, narrow-minded, bigoted God that no sane person would want to love. Their self-defined "family" is their idol, their politics is their idolatry, and their actions fit the Bible's clearest definition of immorality – idolatry.

The Fertility Idol

Strange as it may sound, the fertility idol is still alive. In spite of all the condemnations throughout the Bible, Christians still try to worship fertility. The Roman Catholic Church is by far the most serious promoter of this idolatry, and some of its prelates are among the idol's most avid devotees.

In a world facing serious overpopulation problems, the Roman Church continues to condemn "unnatural" birth control. Why? There is no real logic except that it violates the idol of fertility. Christianity itself has nothing to do with reproduction, one way or the other. Why should reproduction, then, play such a prominent role in the development of Roman Catholic "theology"? It must be the fertility god(dess).

The pronouncements are even more bizarre than simple condemnations of birth control pills and devices (not to be confused with abortion-inducing drugs or devices). The Roman

---

[57] A political group led by Lou Sheldon and headquartered in Anaheim, California, devoted to the worship of the family idol. www.traditionalvalues.org

[58] A political group founded by Donald Wildmon and headquartered in Tupelo, Mississippi, devoted to the worship of the family idol. www.afa.net

[59] A political group founded to oppose marriage equality, headquartered in Washington, D.C., and devoted to the worship of the family idol. www.nationformarriage.org

Church issues complicated theological statements about when it is acceptable for a woman to have a hysterectomy. I remain truly baffled as to why that is any more relevant to theology or morality than when it would be acceptable to have a tonsillectomy. Christianity teaches us that our whole bodies are creations of God. Astarte and the other pagan fertility deities focus on ovaries, uteri, genitalia, and sexual activity. I rest my case in convicting Rome, but I will go on to describe the evil this idolatry produces.

The first and most obvious is economic disaster. Many Roman Catholic countries are poor and trying desperately to develop economically. They are overburdened with people, and in some starvation, or at best malnutrition, is the norm. Having more children is clearly not the answer. Yet the Roman Church continues to condemn international efforts to promote birth control. In doing so, the church is essentially perpetuating poverty and even death. Similar cases could be made with regard to impoverished persons within the United States and other developed countries.

The second case against the anti-birth-control idolatry is that it promotes death. AIDS is a fatal disease that can be transmitted sexually. The disease is transmitted through rather coarse means that are easily defined and easily stopped. Condoms and other means of safe sex (such as sexual activity that does not involve transmission of semen) do work. This is a fact, not an opinion.[60] Technically one does not get AIDS by having sex, but by absorbing fluids.

Children need to be taught from a very early age the facts about AIDS. One of the facts is that relatively simple precautions can and do prevent its transmission. The statement that only abstinence is 100% safe is a lie,[61] and it prevents young people from protecting themselves. I happen to believe that young people would be better off waiting until their

---

[60] I know this is true. My life today is proof. For eleven years I lived in an intimate relationship with a person who has now died of AIDS. During most, if not all, of that relationship, he carried the human immunodefficiency virus (HIV). To this day, I do not. Yet we lived together, slept together, ate together, and had safe sex together throughout this whole eleven years. People that claim safe sex does not work have not bet their life on it. I have, and I have proven them wrong. Furthermore, medical science and common sense are on my side. Abstinence certainly is a way to prevent AIDS transmission, but it is clearly not the only way, nor can it accurately be called the best way.

[61] One of the arguments used to describe condoms' ineffectiveness is the fact that sometimes people forget to use them in the heat of passion. Obviously the same could hold for abstinence. Clearly many people in the heat of passion forget that they had decided to abstain from sex. So by the same logic used against condoms, one would have to argue that abstinence was not 100% effective either.

twenties to explore sexuality. There is so much else to explore before then without all the complications of sex. (This is not because of morality *per se*, but just because it seems like a more optimal way to grow in education, insight, economic potential, etc.) Regardless, we know that all young people do not follow that ideal pattern. Given that fact, we owe the children the facts that will help them stay healthy. It is sinful to hold back information about condoms because they are "unnatural birth control," just like it is sinful to withhold from them detailed information about the sexual mechanics of AIDS transmission just because it involves graphic discussions of types of sex that some people would like to ignore.

So the false idols of fertility and family stand hand-in-hand on this issue. Roman prelates vigorously condemn condom distribution in schools. Fundamentalists oppose sex education. These idolatries go on promoting death and disguising their gross immorality with the veneer of virtue. It is unconscionable that supposed Christians would allow AIDS to continue to be spread just because of their idolatrous worship of procreation and/or "traditional values."

The Deception Idol

Closely related to the family idol is the idol of deception. Simply put, this idol encourages all kinds of immoral and unethical behavior by letting people confuse sex or various forms of sex with immorality itself. Even popular language reflects that deception. Many people, even those only nominally involved in their religion, confuse the term "immorality" with "sexual impropriety." If someone is described as an "immoral woman," many people would immediately think of a prostitute, or at least a person who led a promiscuous life. Yet nothing was said about this woman's sexual habits. She could, in fact, be a celibate virgin who robbed banks, murdered her neighbor, or lied to everyone she met. In fact, I would argue that such a bank robber, murderer, or habitual liar was probably more immoral than the prostitute or the promiscuous woman concocted in people's minds.

This is the work of the deception idol, which has carefully set itself up in popular opinion. Because of this idol, all kinds of immorality are allowed to run rampant in our society. Neighborhoods may band vigorously together to shut down an "adult" bookstore, while the same neighborhood may do nothing to stop gang violence or may turn the other way when a neighbor brutally abuses his spouse because it is "not their concern." Parents are outraged if one child in a school is "fondled," but they willingly ignore a hundred who drop out or fail. Likewise, communities may complain that they have insufficient police personnel or budgets to control crime, while in the same community one could find undercover police officers patrolling parks and other public areas to control "vice." Simply put, truly heinous crimes may go unchecked simply because they are not sexual. Neighborhoods and communities such as these are neither reacting rationally nor morally, but are demonstrating that they have fallen into the subtle grasp of the idol of deception.

Likewise in personal life, the people who are often most concerned with sexual propriety often fail to see their own immorality, simply because it is not sexual. Politicians who champion "family values" have been known to be involved in buyouts and other forms of political corruption. Yet even recently politicians have been essentially ruined because of a minor sexual indiscretion. Recently,[62] presidential candidate Gary Hart was eliminated from the race because he admitted to having had an extramarital sexual affair with a woman. Yet former presidential aide Oliver North ran a close race for a seat in the Senate when it is common knowledge that he lied to Congress with regard to the Iran-Contra scandal. Conservative Evangelicals were responsible for the demise of Gary Hart and the popularity of Oliver North. Yet one must clearly ask the question of which is more relevant for high government office, having had an extramarital affair or having lied to Congress. The answer seems trivially obvious to me.

Little did we know at the first writing of this book that the example would get even more graphic when President Bill Clinton was impeached in 1998 for having oral sex with an intern. (Some would say for lying under oath, but people lie in court under oath all the time, even when they plead "not guilty" to a traffic violation when they know full well they are guilty. I do not believe for a moment that Bill Clinton would have been impeached if he had lied about something not sexual.) We spent millions of dollars and our government became obsessed with Monica Lewinsky's DNA-stained dress. Yet Ronald Reagan either knew about the Iran-Contra affair, in which case he was corrupt, or did not know about it, in which case

---

[62] In 1988, *i.e.* "recently" at this book's first edition, though the problem persists to this day.

he was inept. The idea that Clinton, and not Reagan, was impeached, shows the idol of deception at work in our society.

"Christian" businessmen, who may well champion conservative social causes in the name of their religion, are not necessarily known for exemplary business ethics. A parent who discovers that his teenager has been sexually active may respond with physical abuse. By concentrating so heavily on sexual matters, these people trick themselves into believing that they are leading moral lives. Because they have never cheated on their spouse and were virgins when they got married, they can rationalize all sorts of nonsexual immorality, simply by not thinking of the behaviors as "immoral."

It is relatively easy to see that the priority is a bit confused. This deception has become so destructive because it has diverted our attention away from important matters. Even in the Church itself the problem has made itself known. As Michael Frost, the Ecumenical Catholic Bishop of New York, once put it, "If I preached from the pulpit that there were really four Persons in the Trinity, the average person would dismiss it is some new theology and would not be bothered, but if I announce that I married two lesbians, people get upset. People have entirely lost hold of the hierarchy of Truth, confusing the vital with the unimportant, and the unimportant with the vital." This is further evidence of the idolatry of deception that has permeated modern society.

The Selfishness Idol

The idol of self, which permeates modern society as much as the family idol, is certainly not exclusively related to sexual issues. However, it is just as certainly involved in them.

We have discussed many of the immoral behaviors that this idol brings about with relation to sexuality. Primarily, those who worship themselves tend to not care about the others involved in a sexual encounter. These others include (a) the other partner(s), (b) any potential children which could result from the encounter, (c) one's own spouse, and (d) the spouses of the other partner(s). If any of these people are ignored during the consideration of whether or not to engage in a sexual encounter, then the idol of self is being worshipped.

Note that it is not the sex itself that is the immorality, but rather the failure to consider the wills and desires of others. Rape is an extreme case (although rape is often not truly a sexual offence, but one of violence and control). At least as crucial, but sometimes dismissed by society as less important, is the lack of concern for potential children. In heterosexual encounters, this consideration is always a necessary prerequisite to a morally upright sexual encounter. If either the man or the woman is not ready to raise a resultant child, and if there is a possibility that pregnancy may occur, then sex cannot be entered into without slipping into selfish idolatry, and hence immorality.

In cases of unwanted pregnancy, the relationship between the man and woman (ranging from a stable marriage to an act of prostitution) is essentially irrelevant if the child is not wanted. It is sinful to bring an unwanted child into the world. Obviously, it is even more sinful to abort a pregnancy and kill a child just because the child is not wanted.

The idolatrous selfish attitude is present in both men and women. In men, it appears with "it's her responsibility." There are actually men who believe that the children they father are primarily the responsibilities of the women. Even though this view is clearly selfish, blatantly sexist, and "politically incorrect" in the strongest sense, it is surprisingly common. Some men are open about this belief. No doubt far more keep these beliefs hidden but act upon them nonetheless.

In women, the attitude is most predominant in the insistence upon the right to "choose" whether to be pregnant. Of course there is a right to choose, but that right is morally exercised before intercourse, not after. Most abortions are done for extremely selfish, and thus idolatrous and immoral, reasons. Having an abortion because one's career would be hampered, because it would affect a family's economic stability, or because someone "isn't ready for" children or does not want another child is just an appearance of the idol of self.

The Recreation Idol

The sexual idolatry that will be most readily accepted by conservative Christians is the recreation idol. It is fairly common in modern society, but perhaps not as common as would first be thought. Furthermore, it is important that we realize that this idol is not exclusively sexual, but rather that sexuality is but one of the many modes it takes.

In its basic form, the idol of recreation supplants the True God as the primary object of worship in a person's life. The sexual side of this idol shows itself when someone chooses to neglect public worship because s/he was out Saturday night seeking and/or practicing sex. Note that the sin, however, is not the sex itself (whatever form it may have been), but rather the failure to show up to Sunday worship. The sexual facet of this idol is neither better nor worse than its other multitude of facets. Suppose John spends every Saturday night at bars seeking sex and either goes home with someone or else comes home so late and hung-over that he does not go to worship on Sunday morning. Suppose Jane works so hard during the day, and puts in so much Saturday overtime, that Sunday morning is her only morning to sleep in. Suppose Tim uses Sunday morning as the one day he has to take his children on outings. Suppose Judy is an avid sports fan and spends Sunday morning watching football, baseball, hockey, basketball, or whatever else may be on television. As far as the idol of recreation is concerned, John is no better or worse than Jane, Tim, or Judy. All four of them have let something (sex, work, family, sports, or whatever) take the rightful place of God in their lives. That is idolatry.

This sort of idolatry is rampant in our Western culture. We must be careful not to miss the point in John's case. While we can rightfully condemn such sexual abuses, we should be careful to condemn the other nonsexual abuses as well.

Natural Law

As the Roman Catholic Church becomes more involved in the moral debate over sexuality, one encounters the medieval concept of "natural law." It is a most unusual concept and it is not at all what its name implies. In other words, it is really not about "nature" as we know it. Rather, it is some convoluted estimate of what human nature is *supposed* to be – what God wants us to be rather than what we actually are – and thus supposed to apply universally to all human society. While Thomas Aquinas and others of his time may have believed this ideal was reflected in objective nature, we now know that his beliefs about sexuality were no more consistent with actual nature than was the Church's view of the earth-centered universe. The intrinsic problem with "natural law" is that there is nothing intrinsic about it, in spite of its common assertions that various acts are intrinsically good or evil. "Natural law," therefore, is neither natural nor rational.

One could develop, for example, a rational argument that murder was intrinsically evil. Life is what we value the most (an obvious point). Taking the life of another deprives that person of that basic value. Murder, taking another's life, is therefore intrinsically evil. It destroys the other's life regardless of what the various participants may think and regardless of what their intents or motivations are. The same cannot be said, for example, of adultery. Consider a married couple who both desire to have an affair and make an agreement to let each other have one single-night extramarital sexual encounter. The couple themselves view this as uplifting and beneficial to their marriage. They are open and honest with the people with whom they have the affairs. Everything is straightforward and there are no hard feelings. "Natural law" would consider this "intrinsically evil," but how can one possibly argue that the "evil," if any at all, is *intrinsic*? Unlike murder, which robs a person of life regardless of anyone's motivations or thoughts, the harm from adultery is solely in the mind of the beholder. The persons involved are free to determine for themselves whether or not they feel harmed by the actions. Some will; some won't, unlike murder victims, who are by definition 100% dead.

The odd concept of "natural law" is what enables the Roman Church to be even more idiosyncratic on sexual issues than the Protestant fundamentalists. This is why things such as artificial birth control – which are not discussed one way or the other in Scripture and hence cannot even be misinterpreted from Scripture – enter into Roman moralism but not Protestant moralism.[63]

The first thing to realize is that "natural law" is not based on nature. Many people don't understand that. When they hear, for example, that homosexuality violates "natural law" they accept on face value that this is because animals were designed to be heterosexual or that heterosexuality exists because of reproduction of the species.

Of course these statements themselves are not correct. There are several ways in which reproduction exists other than heterosexuality. Simple organisms reproduce asexually, by splitting in two. Even some higher plants do this – sending shoots from roots or fallen or cut branches growing into the ground. Others reproduce sexually but not heterosexually. A snail, for example, is both male and female. Any two snails can mate with each other and reproduce sexually. An individual snail can even mate with itself (so don't think your garden is safe just because you have only one snail). There is no intrinsic universal principal that would have prevented humans and other vertebrates from having been created the same way. But, human beings for the most part (but not entirely, as discussed above) exist as discrete males and females and biological reproduction usually involves at least one of each.

We have already discussed the problems with assuming that sexuality can only serve reproductive purposes in a morally upright manner. We have also alluded to the fact that heterosexual monogamy is virtually unknown among nonhuman mammals (most of which are very promiscuous and many of which form long-term same-sex bonds).

---

[63] The concept of "natural law" is extremely difficult for modern people to grasp because it is so far removed from our concepts of science, nature, and law. Although I disagree with many of his conclusions, I found the writings of Dr. James Hanigan, professor of moral theology at Duquesne University, Pittsburgh, Pennsylvania, helpful in getting at least a hint of this bizarre concept. See his essay "Unitive and Procreative Meaning: The Inseparable Link" appearing in *Sexual Diversity and Catholicism* edited by Patricia Jung and Joseph Coray (Collegeville, MN: The Liturgical Press, 2001). Another interesting commentary is provided by Jewish blogger Noah Millman in his essay "What's Natural about Natural Law" found in The American Conservative (http://www.theamericanconservative.com/millman/whats-natural-about-natural-law/). He describes how the rabbinic regulations regarding kosher dishes were based on science of the time but science which is no longer understood to be accurate, yet the Orthodox insist that the rules remain as they were even though they are scientifically inaccurate and even considering that they were developed by trying to apply then-accepted science to the underlying principles.

But "natural law" in Roman Catholic thinking is not really related to nature. Therefore (unfortunately) it is not disprovable by pointing out that nature includes such things as parthenogenic female lizards and life-long homosexual male dolphin couples.

As best I understand it (and I admit that it is a very difficult concept to understand because it is so contrary to modern science) "natural law" somehow equates sexuality with the creative power of God and thereby following this natural law becomes part of what it means to be created in God's image. To some extent it derives from the misunderstanding of Genesis that Adam rejoiced in Eve's femaleness rather than her humanness (see above).

Again it seems obvious to point out that in real nature procreation itself is not always connected with sexuality, and even when sexual not always heterosexual as we know it. But we miss the point because the medieval concept was not derived by modern science observing the physical world in spite of the term "natural."

Natural law proponents cite not only Adam and Eve, but also Genesis 1:27, "In the image of God He created them; male and female He created them." In spite of the fact that conservative Catholic theologians would never conceive of God as a sexual being, and cringe at the thought of using feminine terminology to refer to God, they somehow think that "male and female" together is vital to humanity's creation in God's image. This is again a misunderstanding of Genesis. The point is simply that all men *and* women are equally *individually* representative of God's image (since God is genderless), not that it somehow takes *both* a man and woman to fully represent God.

Yet herein lies the idolatry. It is called "complementarity" – the idea that God is only imaged within humanity when male and female are present. If this concept were not so damaging and so idolatrous it would be simply laughable, yet it stands at the core of the repression of over a billion of God's people. To say that God is only represented through both male and female is as silly as saying God is only represented through both black and white. Clearly white and black people equally represent the image of God (as do all other races). And one could argue that God's full diversity is only represented by the fullness of human diversity – black, white, yellow, brown, straight-haired, curly-haired, brown-eyed, blue-eyed, etc. In like manner you could argue that only the fully complement of the human race, male and female, feminine and masculine, represents God in fullness. One never could or should argue that God's creativity can only (or even best) be represented by the union of male and female. If we want to do that, logic would take it to the extreme that God was only fully represented by the union of a smart, able-bodied, black-haired African with a dim-witted, handicapped, blond European (or any other odd combination of opposites.) The concept of "complementarity" simply does not hold up to logical scrutiny.

Yet is causes the obsession with reproduction. It causes the association of divine creativity with biological reproduction, in spite of the fact that there are many, many other ways that human beings mirror the divinely creative activities of God.

When one grasps this odd concept, one can finally see why artificial birth control is banned. (I never did understand this until I read up on "natural law" since I came from a biblically based repressive religious background.) It somehow inhibits the union of male and female in a creative act and thereby somehow circumvents God's ability to create. Talk about binding God with human chains!

"Natural law" is the same system that caused the Church to reject astronomical science because "the earth must be the center of the universe since the universe's Creator was born on earth in Bethlehem." It simply lacks logical connection to either good science or good theology. It is high time the Roman hierarchy scrapped natural law to the heaps of ancient mistakes. There is no other way to put it.

Natural law and "complementarity" are idolatry because they make God into something He is not. They make God a dualistic male-female being that is more reminiscent of Eastern yin-yang than biblical monotheism.

They are additionally evil because they damage the vast majority of human beings – perhaps even all of us indirectly by their resultant overpopulation of our planet. While biblical fundamentalism tends to restrict its destructive vengeance to various subsets of the population, "natural law" is an equal-opportunity abuser. We must ultimately deal with the Bible and its misinterpretations, but we have no reason at all to be burdened by the bad theories of the middle ages.

Unlike fundamentalism, which is based to some extent on misguided applications of a modern worldview, "natural law" is based on a worldview that is outdated and is difficult either to understand or refute. The best way to deal with "natural law" is to ignore it – for Christians to simply ignore its ranting irrational diatribes and for the Church to discard it and replace it with real science.

Because "natural law" is so irrational, the Roman Church has for the most part lost its voice in the world as a beacon of virtue. If the Church fails to discard this system, it will never be able to lead the people of God forward in moral virtue, and thus will lose a great opportunity to help society be more pleasing to God.

Marriage

Since the first edition of this book in 1992, the concept of equality in marriage has begun to take root in society. Several countries, including Canada, have given same-sex marriages legal status. Many states have "civil unions" or "domestic partnerships" that give the legal (but not emotional) benefits of marriage to same-sex couples. In the beginning of the 21st Century states have one-by-one began to realize that it is unconstitutional to limit marriage to male-female couples and have enacted marriage equality.

In 2013, after twelve states of the United States had legally established marriage equality, the United States Supreme Court threw out a federal law that refused to grant federal benefits to legally married same-sex couples. It also rejected an appeal on technical grounds that resulted in upholding a lower court ruling that California's voter-approved initiative to limit marriage to male-female couples was unconstitutional.[64] It seems only a matter of time when the Supreme Court will have to declare that same-sex marriage is a legal right, just as it did with interracial marriage in 1967 (*Loving v. Virginia*, 388 U.S. 1).

From a Christian point of view, marriage is a sacrament. There are seven traditional sacraments in the Christian Church. Two of these – Baptism and Communion – are the primary sacraments. They are the ones that are normative of the Christian life. They define what a Christian is – a person who is baptized into the Church and becomes the Body of Christ through the mysteries of the Eucharistic Meal. They are the two sacraments recognized by Protestants as well as Catholics.

The other five sacraments (called "rites" in some churches to distinguish them from the two essential sacraments) are confirmation, marriage, ordination, penance, and anointing of the sick. Three of these – confirmation, marriage, and ordination – are rites of commitment derived from the baptismal covenant (the most important commitment of a Christian's life). Marriage, therefore, at its sacramental, essential nature, is a commitment.

---

[64] The trial court's 136-page ruling in *Perry v. Schwarzenegger* (available online from the *New York Times* at http://documents.nytimes.com/us-district-court-decision-perry-v-schwarzenegger) contains detailed explanations as to limiting marriage to different-sex couples is discriminatory, unconstitutional, and serves no valid state purpose.

The purpose of the sacraments is to enhance the individual Christian and the Kingdom of God. Confirmation, marriage, and ordination must first and foremost be understood in this manner. If this is not their purpose, then they have no business being celebrated in the church.

Christian marriage enhances the Church of Christ because two baptized Christians can sometimes become better servants of Christ as a team than they could as individuals. It is a classic case of being "greater than the sum of the parts." Two electric generators synchronized together in tandem can provide a stronger and more stable power supply than the two can by operating separately. The same is often true of people.

Remember the story of Adam and Eve, the prototypical married couple. Adam was delighted that Eve was the same as he – *i.e.*, human. The Bible called Eve `ezer, "helper." The essential purpose of Eve's creation was not that she and Adam could produce children (remember, God had already created snails and any two snails can mate with each other, and one snail can also mate with itself). The essential purpose of Eve was that she and Adam could be each other's helpers, companions. Whether Adam and Eve were black or white, male or female, etc., was not important. The two worked together.

So the purpose of marriage at its very core is for the two people to become a team. This is for their own good, the good of the world, the good of the Church, and the good of God. Marriage can help us fulfill the basic human quality of being created in God's image – helping to create a wonderful and delightful world full of love.

This is why God honors the commitment of marriage. This is why it is a sacrament. This is why the Church blesses it. This is why the church should only marry couples that are good complements to one another. (Yes, I know I came close to using that dreaded word from "natural law," but I use it in the understanding of good psychology, not bad metaphysics.)

Note that it has absolutely *nothing* to do with sex or gender! Two men, two women, or a man and a woman can just as well form a good marital dyad so long as they are mutually acceptable complements to each other. It has much more to do with mindset than body parts. It is a matter of fitting together emotionally, not of body parts fitting together mechanically. There are good marriages, there are lifeless marriages, and there are bad marriages. Same-sex and different-sex pairs are equally capable of entering into any of these three. Only the first (good marriages) are pleasing to God and beneficial to society.

I actually tend to believe that children are best off raised by a married couple. I am happy that my parents remained married. I do not believe parents should stay together just for the sake of the children, because such forced continuation of a dangerous or violent marriage is probably worse than the option of separation. Nonetheless, the "family values" proponents are probably right in the concept that a two-parent family provides a more nurturing environment for raising children.

Nothing is said, though, about it being one male and one female. That is as irrelevant as any other aspect of the people's lives. One could probably argue that the marriage of an auto mechanic and a professor would be a more balanced environment for child-raising since it would combine and balance the benefits of a vocational and an academic background (regardless of the sex or sexual orientation of the mechanic or professor). But one would hardly argue that only people from different occupational or socioeconomic backgrounds should be allowed to marry. The argument that only different-sex couples should raise children is equally preposterous.

We might do well to visit again the typical social structure of the bottle-nosed dolphin, regarded as one of our closest counterparts on the intellectual scale. Most males form life-long homosexual pair bonds. They mate with females "in season," and the calves (whether male or female) are raised by the females. This is nature at work. It is "natural law" in some sense of the term. While this does not mean it is the "ideal model," it does negate the idea that the male-female pair-bond raising their own offspring is the only proper or God-given model for humans to follow. (God did, after all, create dolphins and presumably did not set them up in a system where they did something naturally that He considered sinful or disgusting.)

The Church betrays its own theology when it limits marriage to different-sex couples. Either marriage is a sacrament or it is not. If it is a sacrament, it is for the purpose of uplifting the Body of Christ. The companionship and teamwork of two men or two women is just as able to build up the Body of Christ as is that of a man and a woman. Both history and present society are full of abundant examples that substantiate this fact.

If marriage is not a sacrament and serves only the purpose of procreation, then the Church ought not be in the marriage business at all. People can and do procreate quite well without either the Church or the state helping them. If having children is the purpose of marriage, the Church should stop holding marriage services and the state should stop giving marriage licenses.

Since procreation is not the primary purpose of marriage (even though it is one benefit of it), the Church should marry qualified same-sex couples and qualified different-sex couples. Rather than limiting marriage licenses to different-sex couples, the state should establish meaningful criteria (such as economic or emotional stability perhaps) before it grants marriage licenses to couples. Not every pair is qualified for marriage, but the qualifications have little if anything to do with the sex of the partners.

Likewise we should note carefully that marriage is not primarily a legal arrangement nor is its primary purpose the protection and/or social welfare of either spouse. These are important and valuable results of marriage, but they are not its purpose. They miss the emotional component of the concept of "helper" and "companion."

There is a tendency in the gay community and the liberal aspects of society in general to legalize such concepts as "domestic partnership" and "civil union." Perhaps this is a step forward, as it enables long-term same-sex couples to enjoy some, most, or all of legal benefits as marriage different-sex couples. But unless it is called "marriage" it will never have the full component of emotional benefits allocated to married different-sex couples.

All of the legal benefits, no matter how important they be, are essentially things that can be bought with money. Marriage is far too important to be reduced to such a trivial level. What is most important is not inheritance rights but the social acceptance that will come when someone says to a stranger "I got married yesterday" and the stranger has to wonder whether he married a man or a woman, or when a person talks about her son-in-law and her friend asks whether she meant Bill or Sue's husband.

People do not go around saying "I got domestic partnered" or "I got civil unioned"; they say "I got married." No matter how close a legal parallel is established, it is not the same unless we call it what it is – marriage.

In the Ecumenical Catholic Church we recognize the full equivalence of same-sex and opposite-sex marriage. The liturgy is the same for either one,[65] and the term "marriage" is used as long as the two partners are baptized Christians, since baptism is the one and only qualification for participation in the other sacraments. We do not use substitutional phrases such as "holy union" or "civil union." We perform the same ceremony regardless of whether the state recognizes the relationship because God, not the state, is the arbiter of sacramental grace. We have thus set the tone for the full equality of marriage and based our sacraments upon sound theology rather than mistaken social customs. Society, like all of life, constantly evolves, and eventually this will become the norm throughout the world.

---

[65] There are optional Old Testament lessons for the three basic marriage types – gay male, lesbian, and heterosexual. Interestingly, the Old Testament story about heterosexual *love* (as opposed to property-based marriage) was the most difficult to find and is actually from the Apocrypha, while the male-male love story (Jonathan and David) and the female-female love story (Naomi and Ruth) are from the primary canon of the Old Testament.

Conclusion

We have explored a wealth of information on the Bible, sexuality, and salvation. Hopefully you have been reassured that God's Love is free, and not a result of doing good or being "pure." It is a tough struggle to erase years of old, negative tapes; we hope that this book will help you do that.

Post Script: *Sancta Mater Ecclesia*

Emotional Relationship with the Church

Today, almost twenty years after Jeffery and I first undertook the endeavor of writing this book, it seems necessary to tackle another topic which had not been adequately discussed, and that is the role of "Holy Mother Church" in the lives of so many people. This additional topic has become more readily apparent as we are preparing a Spanish translation that will hopefully be widely published and used in Mexico and other Latin American countries. While the recent history of the United States has shown much exposition of erroneous biblical interpretations related to sexuality, sadly such has not been the case within Spanish literature.

I was raised a Lutheran, went to Episcopalian seminary, and became active in independent Catholic ministry. Jeffery was a life-long Episcopalian who sometimes attended Baptist churches and was active in the Metropolitan Community Church. What I have learned in the course of these years in dealing with "cradle" Catholics is that there is a strong emotional component to Catholicism that is simply missing and frankly quite foreign to us raised in Protestantism, even in "high church" liturgical Protestant denominations. My movement toward Catholicism was intellectual, studying the liturgy, theology of the Eucharist, and even intercession of the saints. Obviously I was aware of the common translation of Mary being *Theotokos* (Greek for "God-Bearer") as "*Mater Dei*" or "Mother of God," but for me it still remained what I believe to be the original intent of the Ecumenical Council – a *Christological statement about Jesus being truly God,* rather than a statement saying something about the nature of His mother Mary. Furthermore, it never occurred to me that whatever anyone thought about Mary had an emotional component, any more than I thought of God the Father in the same emotional terms as I think of Kenneth Shirey, my human father (all of which emotions are positive as I have a very congenial and loving father), or that Jeffery had toward his abusive human father.

Clearly religion is emotional, but for us of Protestant upbringing I would suggest that this emotional component is transient in nature. We are moved by a Bach chorale, brought to heavenly bliss by great liturgy, inspired by a moving sermon. Yet this is akin to the emotions one might have when one's national anthem is sung or one's favorite sports team wins a game. It is something that dissipates soon after the emotion's initiating event. These are not the emotions I am here discussing. Rather I am discussing the relationship-based emotions that Roman Catholics have toward the Church, or more specifically toward the institution of the Roman Catholic Church. (Even Roman Catholics who know better at an intellectual level often fail to distinguish emotionally between the Roman Catholic denomination represented by the Vatican and the Universal Church, the Body of Christ, of which the Vatican-based institution is only one of many parts.)

The difference between this emotionally-based Catholic relationship to the Church and the intellectually-based Protestant relationship to the Church is all wrapped up in the concept of *Sancta Mater Ecclesia*, "Holy Mother Church." While Protestants are encouraged to have a "personal relationship" with Jesus Christ – to view Him as Lord, King, God, Savior, and even "Brother" – they rarely if ever think of the Church in terms of human familial relations. Even biblical concepts such as the "Bride of Christ" are thought of simply as metaphors that are useful to help us make sense of something beyond true comprehension.

"Mother Church" is not a new term to me, but it has become quite apparent that my Protestant-turned-Catholic grasp of the term missed much of the point. "God is our Father, the Church is our mother." It is still just a convenient analogy, an ability to comprehend these spiritual relationships through human approximations, and like all divine anthropomorphisms, these approximations are never meant to be anything close to reality, though for many they may have felt that way.

Note also that I used a small "m" in calling the Church our "mother." There would be no reason for an intellectually based understanding to capitalize that "m" any more than we would capitalize the "i" in "it" when speaking of the Church (and we Protestant-intellectual English-speakers would never use "she" or "he" for the Church because it is an inanimate organization, just like our high school or our social club or our nation).

Yet lifelong Catholics routinely refer to the Church as "she." I have come to realize that this is more than simply a quirky translation of Latin which, like Spanish and French, uses gendered pronouns for all sorts of inanimate objects. In English we would not call a table "she" in spite of it being "*la mesa*" in Spanish and taking feminine adjectives and pronouns. Likewise with the Church, except for lifelong Catholics.[66]

My contention is that this terminology reflects a very deep emotional understanding of the Church, and furthermore that this emotional connection may provide an additional layer of discord to lifelong Catholics wrestling with issues of sexuality.

It is for this reason that I am adding this postscript, an additional chapter to address this subject. One approach would be to try to integrate it into the book. However, the discussion of Scripture remains essentially untouched by this emotional component, and thus this chapter is best left as a separate entity.

Abusive Parent

Some aspects related to the "Holy Mother Church" issue have already been discussed. For example, the Roman Church depends on the same Bible as do the Orthodox and Protestant churches. The discussions of biblical interpretation – and misinterpretation – remain the same. To some extent the importance of these discussions is even displaced by the emotional emphasis on the Church as "controlling mother" as opposed to "authoritative teacher." We may agree or disagree with a teacher's application of science, mathematical calculations, or artistic interpretations, and in challenging our teacher's presentation, we would cite other scientific research, review mathematical derivations, or even read about an artist's own description of his art. The challenges we would make to our own mother's

---

[66] I realize that in the Spanish translation, as well as translations into any other languages that lack neuter pronouns, this distinction will seem foreign, so I will attempt to explain again. In Spanish one might say "*Ella es una mujer bonita y ella es una mesa bonita*." That would be translated into English as "**She** is a beautiful woman and **it** is a beautiful table." Notice that the Spanish pronoun *ella* is translated as "it" for the table and "she" for the woman. It would not be proper to use "she" in both parts of the sentence. In fact, if a word-for-word translation produced the sentence "**She** is a beautiful woman and **she** is a beautiful table" many English-speakers would simply envision one object, the woman, perhaps lying on her back with dishes or flowers or food set on top of her. The idea of using "she" to describe a table is so bizarre that in hearing that improper translation one would conjure up odd images that simply were not implied by the original Spanish sentence. The same is true with regards to the Church. *Ecclesia* is a feminine word in Latin. It takes feminine Latin pronouns. That does not mean, however, that it is appropriate to use "she" or "her" when referring to the Church in English. Doing so is the linguistic equivalent of the above mistranslation where a table is called "she." Official English translations promulgated by the Vatican continue to make this translation error and this – at least in English-speaking peoples – perpetuates an erroneous and excessively emotional perception of the institution of the Church.

directions are not so based on logic. If our mother told us not to cross the street, we are unlikely to cite (even if as children we had the skills) average vehicle speeds and accident statistics as evidence, even if such facts would be supportive of our desire to cross the street. Rather we are faced with two choices – obedience leading to not crossing the street, or disobedience that gets us across the street but risks (a) punishment, (b) the fear of punishment even if unrealized, or (c) guilt for having misbehaved, even if or perhaps more likely if, punishment were not our particular parents' normal *modus operandi*. Thus we are in a lose-lose situation of having to choose between obedience that circumvents our desires or disobedience that has negative consequences.

Through the course of history, the Roman Church has developed many convoluted and bizarre justifications for some of its moral positions. "Natural law" is one of them, though admittedly the earlier discussion was intellectual in nature and was an attempt to understand Roman Catholic concerns without addressing, or even being aware of, this underlying emotional component of the relationship of Catholics to their church. (As an aside that I cannot resist making, but will not explore further as it is not germane to the subject of this book – there is no more convoluted twisting of logic and theology than Rome's arguments against female clergy. The argument that Jesus was male and priests represent Jesus simply bears no logic unless we require all priests to be native-born Jews born in Bethlehem and terminate their ministry when they reach 33 years of age [perhaps by early retirement as opposed to crucifixion]. If the Roman church wishes to have sexist rules regarding ordination, perhaps that is its prerogative, but it should not hide behind illogical and made-up "theology" for its justification.)

The issue of concern here, however, is the relationship between a living person of Roman Catholic upbringing who is trying to reconcile personal sexuality with the teachings of the Roman Catholic Church and the Church itself. This is particularly difficult because of the Roman Church's unique obsession with sexual issues. For Protestants the erroneous sexual teachings are mostly limited to homosexuality, pre-marital and extra-marital sex. For Roman Catholics one must add divorce and birth control to that list.[67] Thus the spectrum of Roman

---

[67] At an emotional level abortion would be included in this list of sexual sins, even though abortion is not a sexual sin but rather an issue of the sanctity of life. The loose connection with sexuality may explain the logical inconsistency between the Roman Church's greater focus on abortion than the death penalty. At a logical level,

Catholics abused by their church for sexual issues is even broader than that of most Protestant denominations.

In fact, Rome's teachings put even the so-called "traditional family" at risk of violation if that family chooses to be socially responsible in our over-populated and over-polluted world by using birth control. (I would argue that it is immoral *not* to use some form of birth control in the vast majority of sexual encounters and that a true sexual morality based upon love and logic would focus first and foremost on whether the act might lead to the conception of a child and, if so, whether that is best for both the potential child and the world as a whole. One can easily deduce from this basis of sexual morality that the concerns for heterosexual encounters might be far more stringent and complex than for homosexual encounters. Furthermore, irresponsible heterosexuality is sinful not directly in itself but because it can lead to several serious sins including abortion, giving birth to an unwanted and/or unloved child, and contributing to the world's strangling population growth.)

From my work counseling many Roman Catholics struggling through issues of sexuality, I have observed that many times their behavior and attitude toward the Roman Church is similar to the behavior and attitude of abused children toward their abusive parents. It is a love-hate relationship that is difficult to break. This becomes most clear when a native-born Roman Catholic struggles with moving to a different church. It goes far beyond doctrinal teachings about being the "real church" and delves into an emotional arena. One salient example that comes to mind is when I was talking to a divorced and remarried woman who was concerned that her church rejected her. I suggested that she become an Episcopalian (there was not an Ecumenical Catholic parish in her area). I pointed out to her that worship in an Episcopal church is essentially the same as the Roman Mass and that she would feel very much at home. She didn't raise questions about apostolic succession or the validity of sacraments. She didn't ask about the Pope. She didn't cite Roman canon law. She didn't rant about Henry VIII or the Reformation. She didn't really come up with any concerns of the head, but just sort of had a bewildered "I'm not sure I could leave my church" feeling. When I met her again a year or so later she had simply quit attending church but still considered herself to be a "Catholic."

---

if politicians are excommunicated for supporting abortion rights, they should certainly also be excommunicated for supporting the death penalty.

It was through her that I first sensed that my suggestion to her to become an Episcopalian was about the same as if I had suggested to Jeffery that he forget about his abusive father (who had died in Viet Nam) and simply consider my kind-hearted father as his own real father. Jeffery did love my father, and vice versa, but that did not erase Jeffery's deep-seated emotional issues connected to the abusive past relationship with his natural father. I suspect that for many Roman Catholics who leave the Roman church in favor of more accepting denominations there may still remain the haunting turmoil caused by the abusive parental relationship of "Holy Mother Church" focused on sexual repression.

When a person goes to therapy to deal with abusive parents, the therapist uses intellectual training to help the patient through emotional issues. The same is necessary here, and we will approach this emotional issue with some intellectual resources to help mitigate the devastating effects of the abuse. I do not expect the rationality to immediately counterbalance the emotional hurt (though I would hope it does). It may well be something that takes years to work through, as abuse issues often do.

As with most emotional problems, the first step is realization. Hopefully people reading this will become aware of the possibility of the Church functioning as an emotionally abusive parent, especially among people who have a "parental" relationship with their church. Perhaps the discussion of the basic Protestant-Catholic difference in views of the Church has been helpful. Perhaps it has confused you because you happen to be a Catholic who views the Church intellectually as an institution or a Protestant who thinks of the Church as your "mother." There is not and never has been a black-and-white dichotomy between "Catholic" and "Protestant" whatever those terms may mean. Martin Luther and John Calvin were, after all, Catholics. The point is not to distinguish Catholicism and Protestantism, but rather to point out the underlying issues of institutional versus parental relationships with the Church, both the worldwide Church and its representation at the local level.

I would suggest that if you read through various discussions on sexuality and morality, what the Bible does and doesn't say (including previous chapters of this book), and still are wrestling with whether or not God loves you, you are perhaps seeing God through the eyes of a parental church. Perhaps it is akin to your mother saying, "Grandma wouldn't approve of you doing _____."

So now I will step back into my intellectual mode and put on my "therapist hat" and point out why the Church is *not* your mother and you do not have an obligation to please the Church just because you love God. We will, when necessary, delve into Roman canon law, the *Catechism of the Catholic Church*, and Sacred Scripture for support.

Scripture and Tradition

The relationship between Scripture and Tradition is complex and is one of the significant theological differences between the Roman Catholic Church and most Protestant denominations. Establishment of a "proper" relationship between the two is not necessary for the sake of this treatise because both Scripture and Tradition must be challenged with regard to the way they are used to misinterpret human sexuality and mistreat people within the churches. Nonetheless, some understanding will shed a bit of light on why the official teachings of the Church are perhaps more important to Roman Catholics while the exact words of the Bible are more important to Protestants.

The Bible is the foundation of the Church, and yet it is the Church that in fact defined the Bible – *i.e.* it is the councils of the early Church that said "yes" or "no" to whether any particular writing or "book" would be part of the official Bible.[68] In many ways it is similar to the relationship between a nation and its constitution. The constitution may be the "supreme law of the land" but that is actually a misnomer because a piece of paper cannot rule people without their consent. In democracies the people consistently grant power to the constitution, even if passively by their failure to amend it. In less democratic systems the human "supreme ruler" grants power to the constitution (if it even exists) by choosing to follow it or to change it (or perhaps to ignore it). In all cases, the power resides in some human being(s), not in a piece of paper.

Most Protestants accept the Bible as the ultimate authority without any real understanding of how it developed. Some extreme fundamentalists even have attitudes that effectively have God sitting with a pen and paper (or stylus and stone). This belief system

---

[68] This is particularly useful information when refuting door-to-door heretics who deny the Trinity yet claim the Bible as their authority. The Creeds that elucidate the Trinitarian basis of Christianity were written by the very same ecumenical councils that defined the Bible.

can result in any number of dysfunctions, perhaps the most serious being the shocking pervasiveness of the utter stupidity of denying God's ability to create life through evolution. Curiously, this Bible-blinded ignorance is an almost exact parallel of the conflict between Galileo and the Vatican regarding the solar system's heliocentricity. Meanwhile as the debates of human ignorance go on, the earth continues to revolve around the sun and life continues to evolve on earth. For the purposes of this book's subject, the dysfunction of this Biblical supremacy is the tendency to uphold an outdated and scientifically inaccurate sexual moral system that is perhaps even more harmful emotionally than believing the earth is only 6,000 years old.

In the Roman Catholic system Tradition is essentially given equal weight with Scripture, but the fault lies in the weakness of the implementation of the third leg of the balanced stool of truth – Reason. It is only when Scripture (which is by definition fixed) and Tradition (which is cumulative) are balanced with Reason (which ever grows and evolves with the body of human knowledge) that real Truth can manifest itself. In some ways the problems of the Tradition-based system are harder to recognize and challenge than those of the fundamentalist "*sola Scriptura*" systems because through the course of time they eventually avoid such obvious errors as the denial of evolution, thus the dysfunction is more difficult to perceive. The most blatant error still perpetuated by the Tradition-based system is the prohibition of birth control.

The errors in Tradition are also more difficult to pinpoint because Tradition, regardless of how it is actually defined (if defined concretely at all), is far more voluminous than Scripture and is not necessarily self-consistent.[69] Likewise, even though Tradition tends to be cited in official statements, teachings, and edicts, it is seldom cited specifically in day-to-day life, quite contrary to the role Scripture plays in the life of a Protestant, especially a fundamentalistic one. Thus, rather than a few specific Scriptures needing to be explained and brought into light, there is a general "consensus," even if a false one, about what Tradition actually says.

---

[69] Scripture is also not always self-consistent, as for example Genesis 1 and Genesis 2 which reverse the order of creation of human beings and other animals. This lack of self-consistency is among the strongest pieces of evidence against the concept that God literally wrote the Bible.

A perfect example is the present-day terminology "traditional marriage" or "traditional family." Obviously the Bible does not contain a single concept of marriage. The Old Testament patriarchs were for the most part polygamous, and the New Testament apostles were for the most part single. Even within the history of Christianity the traditions, characteristics, and purposes of marriage have been varied and have in general evolved from rites of property acquisition to the relatively new concept of marriage as an expression of love. To put it bluntly, there is nothing "traditional" about the one-man-one-woman marriage of two heterosexual high school sweethearts who go on to have 2.3 children and live happily ever after. Yet very few people realize this and the majority readily accept the term "traditional marriage" even if they do not consider this an ideal or proscriptive model.

The Roman Catholic Church perpetuates this confusion about Tradition. Official documents written with tens or hundreds of pages of Latin voluminously cite prior tradition. Yet when it reaches the day-to-day parishioner, or even the typical parish pastor, it is reduced to "the tradition of the church is _____" and it goes without further exploration or question, even when that conclusion is dubious or, worse yet, blatantly erroneous. "Traditional marriage" as presently defined is not traditional, and the same is true of many other social statements that get twisted and turned before they reach the minds of the Catholic faithful.

There is yet a third system in which "tradition" overrides "scripture," and this system leads to an ultimately unstable institution. Interestingly, this system is the technical opposite of biblical fundamentalism but sometimes reaches the same damaging and dangerous conclusions, similar to the way that communist and fascist dictatorships, while technical opposites, usually appear more similar than different. This unstable system is best exemplified by the Mormon religion, the so-called "Church of Jesus Christ of Latter-day Saints." The Mormon "prophet" (the president of the religious institution) is given powers and authority that would make a medieval pope jealous. The official declarations of the prophet – a sort of on-going tradition – are given equal weight as Scripture (which for them includes additional writings that their founder added to stand side-by-side with the Bible). To enhance the inherent instability even further, Mormon tradition discards the 2000-year tradition of Christianity and focuses on the 200-year tradition of Mormonism. Thus we have seen in the course of only about 100 years a change from blacks being marked with God's curse to being acceptable as priests and a religion founded by polygamists becoming one of the staunchest political foes of marriage equality. Although the system appears stable because of its present alliance with biblical fundamentalists on certain social issues, it is unlikely that such a system where God can change His mind because of social pressures will ultimately last.

Official Vatican Teachings

The official teachings of the Vatican, as contained in the *Catechism of the Catholic Church* (1994 edition bearing the *imprimi potest* of Joseph Cardinal Ratzinger, Paulist Press, ISBN 0-8091-3434-9) are far more intellectual and accurate than what seems to exist in the hearts of many native Roman Catholics. These teachings do, however, plant the emotional seeds that lead to the abusive quasi-parental relationship many people have with the Church.

For example, in §171 the *Catechism* states, "The Church, 'the pillar and bulwark of truth,' faithfully guards 'the faith which was once for all delivered to the saints.' She [*sic*] guards the memory of Christ's words; it is she [*sic*] who from generation to generation hands on the apostles' confession of faith. As a mother who teaches her children to speak and so to understand and communicate, the Church our Mother teaches us the language of faith in order to introduce us to the understanding and the life of faith."

First we note the inaccurate translation from Latin into English when the personal pronoun "she" is used rather than the proper "it." This error, of course, would not occur in languages such as Spanish and French that lacked neuter pronouns. Furthermore, the *Catechism* presents a useful analogy – "as a mother who teaches her children" – but then needlessly personifies the church in a more direct way by using the erroneous "the Church our Mother teaches us …" The *Catechism* would have been better written (in both Latin and English) by simply saying "As parents who teach their children to speak and so to understand and communicate, the Church teaches us the language of faith in order to introduce us to the understanding and the life of faith." This says the same thing regarding the Church's didactic role without clouding it with erroneous and inappropriate personifications.

The Bible never refers to the Church as our mother. It often refers to the people of Israel or to Jerusalem as the bride or wife of God, and sometimes calls God "Husband" as in Isaiah 54:5, "For your Creator is your Husband, YAHWEH Sabaoth is His Name." (NJB). The Bible also calls Israel an adulteress when the people practiced idolatry.[70]

This marital symbolism is occasionally transferred to the Church as the bride of Christ, but this symbolism is much less prominent than the "bride," "wife," and "whore" references to Israel in the Old Testament. Furthermore, it specifically refers to the heavenly Church, or the "New Jerusalem" and is used as a metaphor. Revelation 21:2 speaks of the heavenly Jerusalem that appeared in John's vision, "I saw the holy city, the new Jerusalem, coming down out of heaven from God, prepared as a bride dressed for her husband." The context is clearly that of the *future* – of heaven – and not a reference to the Church on earth.

In the Letter to the Ephesians (5:25), St. Paul compares human marriage to the relationship between Jesus and the Church. "Husbands, love your wives in the same way that Christ loved the Church and gave His life for it.[71]" Paul goes on to discuss the union of husband and wife and to expound upon the similarities between the marital relationship and that between Christ and the Church. Although it is presented in heterosexual terms, there is no logical reason to assert from this passage that the marriages of two men or two women are not equally symbolized by the relationship between Christ and the Church. In fact, since the relationship between Christ and the Church is clearly *not* one of procreation or even sexuality, the similarities between marriage and the Christ-Church relationship support the concept of the equality between same-sex and different-sex marriage. It is indeed odd that an organization such as the Vatican, entirely controlled by males, would thus interpret the symbolism of its own marriage to Jesus as an argument against gay marriage.

---

[70] The Hebrew word used most frequently in this case is זנה *zanah*, which can mean "adultery" in the sense of a person (usually a woman) having sex with someone other than her spouse, but is so often used to mean "idolatry" that its meaning is often confusing. This, of course, reminds us once again that in the times of the Old Testament sexuality and pagan religion were intimately connected, though one should note that Israel is never called קדשה *qadešah*, the "priest-prostitute" of the pagan temples so often misinterpreted as discussed previously.

[71] This is *Today's English Version*, which correctly translates the Greek to "it." Several translations have "her," which as we have discussed is an inaccurate rendition of the feminine Greek pronoun into English, which properly uses the neuter pronoun "it" for inanimate objects, including organizations and groups of people such as the Church.

More prominent than the "Bride of Christ" symbolism, however, is the "Body of Christ" symbolism for the Church. "Now you are the Body[72] of Christ and individually members of it." (1 Cor 12:27, NRSV). Unlike the "bride" symbolism, which is a direct appropriation of Old Testament language regarding Israel, the "body" symbolism is new to Christianity, relating to the unique incarnational aspects of God-made-Man in Jesus Christ. Thus it is when receiving the Eucharist we hear the ambiguous "Mark [*i.e.*, your own name], the Body of Christ."

Thus the Church is the Body of Christ, it is like a bride (that is, waiting in expectant love) for Christ, and it simply is not called "mother" in the Bible, either directly or through metaphor. It is easy to see how these metaphors became blended as history evolved. "We are the Body, the Church." "The Church is like a bride." "God is our Father." The Church becomes our mother. (Though when you think about the various analogies all together there is something incestuous about the relationships.)

The important point remains, however, to break the dysfunctional emotional bond of an abusive mother. This is easier said than done. I hope it helps to understand intellectually that the "Holy Mother Church" concept is not something that Jesus taught. Jesus spoke consistently of God being His Father and our Father. He called us to be together (that is what "*ek-klesia*" means). He called us to be One as He and the Father are One. He did not speak of any person or institution being our Mother.

With this in mind, let us explore a few more official teachings of the Vatican so that we can grasp their important points without being trapped into the emotional and unnecessary anthropomorphisms that may prevent us from rationally dealing with the Church in our lives.

The *Catechism* (§796) discussed the Church as the bride of Christ. It says, "The Church is the spotless bride of the spotless Lamb," quoting Revelation 22. We must remember that Revelation was speaking of the New Jerusalem. It is a vision of heaven, not a description of the Church on earth. Surely no one would argue that the Christian Church in any of its forms or denominations is "spotless." That would not just be naïve, it would be denial of real

---

[72] Σωμα (*sōma*) in Greek, *corpus* in Latin, both of which are neuter in gender.

history. In Revelation the New Jerusalem *has been made pure* by Christ. This is why it is what is to come – a vision of heaven, not a description either of Israel or the earthly Church.

We must also be careful because this symbolism has an implicit sexual purity that can be oppressive if misunderstood. Remember that "adultery" was almost always a symbol of "idolatry" in the Old Testament references to Israel. When the prophets called Israel a "whore" or "adulterer" they were not discussing sexual infractions, but rather falling away from God and wandering into pagan religion and belief. Thus the symbol of the "spotless bride" is not properly understood to be a woman who is not just a virgin but has never even had a lustful thought, but rather is a symbol of someone fully, completely, and faithfully dedicated to the worship of God. Revelation is obviously playing on the Old Testament symbolism, and in the course of 2,000 years we have lost much of that underlying meaning of using sexual actions as symbols for religious acts. As always, we must be very careful when deriving meaning from ancient symbols belonging to another culture.

The Church as the "spotless bride of Christ" is a beautiful symbol. Like so many, it is something that we can easily picture in our minds and thus add a human dimension to a spiritual relationship. It means that in heaven we – the Body of Christ, the Church, the Assembly (*Ekklesia*) of Believers – will be pure in our worship and our unending love for God. It has nothing to do with sexuality, just as it does not literally mean that we will be wearing a white veil and carrying a bouquet or, even more literally, that all of us somehow will be crawling into this one dress with one bouquet to meet our one Husband Jesus. It is a symbol of pure faith and pure religion.

Mary, Mother of Jesus

The Bible and the Creeds tell us that Jesus was born of the Virgin Mary by the action of the Holy Spirit. This is the miracle of the Incarnation, "the Word became flesh and lived among us." (John 1).

In dealing with the Church as "mother" one cannot avoid coming across the related concept of Mary as "mother," not just of Jesus but of us as the Body of Christ. There is some beauty in that symbolism, but as with the church, it is important not to let it become dysfunctional and overbearing. Mary, daughter of Ann and Joachim, did something unique in all of history – she raised a perfect Child. We must be careful not to assume that looking to Mary as our "mother" means that we are also supposed to be perfect.

First of all, Mary's Child was not perfect because of Mary's abilities as a mother, but because of Jesus's dual Nature as Perfect God and Perfect Man, an ontological fact that is itself the mystery of Incarnation. This is not to say that Mary wasn't a wonderful mother; surely God knew what He was doing when He chose her to be the mother of His Son. It is simply saying that Mary cannot instill perfection in us and, furthermore, that she does not expect to do so.

Second we must address Mary's own perfection. Three doctrines have developed through the course of history that are neither scriptural nor contrary to Scripture. Two of these were officially enshrined by the Vatican – the immaculate conception (that Mary was conceived without sin, not by a virgin birth, but by God's grace) and the assumption (that Mary's body was assumed directly into heaven). Although only officially adopted by the Roman Church in the 19th century, they do nonetheless come from long traditions. The third is the "perpetual virginity" of Mary – the idea that she remained a virgin after Jesus was born. This doctrine has become part of some liturgical prayers such as in the prayer of confession in the Roman Catholic Mass, "…and I ask Blessed Mary, *ever* virgin, …"[73]

It is especially important within the context of this book to discuss the perpetual virginity of Mary. Many people, particularly Roman Catholics, believe that Mary remained a virgin throughout her life. Others believe that she and Joseph had other children after Jesus was born. The Bible does mention "brothers" of Jesus (*e.g.* Mark 3:31), though it is not explicitly clear who these "brothers" were. Some argue they were sons of Joseph by a prior marriage. Others argue that they were cousins. Others say that they were children of Mary and Joseph born after Jesus. Anyone who is adamant one way or the other about this misses the point of Christianity and the importance of the virgin birth.

---

[73] This potentially offensive statement can easily be avoided by simply saying "the" in place of "ever": "I ask Blessed Mary the virgin ..."

As with all theological statements and terms about Mary, they are really *Christological* in nature and are saying something, first and foremost, about Jesus. The point of the virgin birth has nothing to do with Mary's sexuality and everything to do with Jesus's parentage. The point is that God is in a unique and special way the Father of Our Lord Jesus Christ. God is Father of us all, but He is physically the Father of Jesus Christ. This is a statement about the dual Natures of Christ – that "He is God from the Substance of His Father, begotten before all time, and Man from the substance of His mother, born in time."[74]

The point is simple, as Luke's Gospel (1:34-35, NRSV) so clearly explains. In her dialog with the Angel Gabriel, who has just told her she would have a baby, Mary asks, "How can this be, since I am a virgin?" (The Greek original is ἐπει ἄνδρα οὐ γινωσκω – *epei andra ou ginōskō* – "since I have not known a male," or in the Latin Vulgate, "*Quomodo fiet istud quoniam virum non cognosco?*") Gabriel responded, "The Holy Spirit will come upon you, and the Power of the Most High will overshadow you; therefore the Child to be born will be holy; He will be called Son of God."[75]

This – *and only this* – is the point of the doctrine of the virgin birth, that Jesus is the Son of God.

It has nothing to do with Mary's worthiness to be the mother of Jesus. It has nothing to do with Mary's purity. It has nothing to do with whether or not she ever did or didn't commit a sin. It has to do with God being the only Father of Jesus.

It is easy to raise Mary up as a symbol of what a human (especially a woman, but also a man) should be. There is much good in this. She led a life entirely dedicated to God. But it is dangerous to use her sexuality, or lack thereof, as a model. She had a unique role to which we are _not_ called – being the physical mother of God Incarnate. It is for this role that she was a virgin when Jesus was born.[76]

---

[74] The *Quicunque Vult*, or "Athanasian Creed," "*Deus est ex Substantia Patris ante saecula genitus: et homo est ex substantia matris in saeculo natus.*"

[75] Πνεῦμα Ἅγιον ἐπελεύσεται ἐπὶ σέ, καὶ Δύναμις Ὑψίστου ἐπισκιάσει σοι: διὸ καὶ τὸ γεννώμενον Ἅγιον κληθήσεται, Υἱὸς Θεοῦ -- *Pneuma Hagion epeleusetai epi se, kai Dynamis Hypsistou episkiasei soi: dio kai to gennōmenon Hagion klēthēsetai, Huios Theou* – or in the Latin Vulgate, "*Spiritus Sanctus superveniet in te et Virtus Altissimi obumbrabit tibi ideoque et quod nascetur Sanctum vocabitur Filius Dei.*"

[76] One could argue that it is not relevant whether Mary was actually a virgin (*i.e.* one who had *never* had sex) when Jesus was born, but rather what was truly important was that Jesus Himself was not conceived through

There is nothing theologically wrong with believing that Mary was "ever virgin" and that she lived her entire life without having sexual relations at all. However, it *is* wrong to deduce from this that such a life is somehow more exemplary, more holy, more God-blessed than a life that includes sexual relations. Whether or not Mary did have other children or did have sexual relations, it is important to accept that she *could* have had them and still would be the holy mother of our Lord, the Son of God, and that God would still have asked her to bear and raise His Son.

As a side note, it does seem appropriate in this discussion of Mary's sexuality and the possibility of her having other children to also discuss the spurious notion common in many fictitious stories and extra-biblical "gospels" that Jesus Himself had children with Mary Magdalene or anyone else. There <u>is</u> a theological problem with that possibility, and this is why Christian Faith categorically declares that Jesus was never married and never had children. If he did have children, they would be demigods of sorts, half True God and fully True Man. From the standpoint of the Incarnation it does not make sense that God would allow this to happen. Furthermore, it would counteract the notion that "all people are created equal" as it would establish a set of human beings who had God the Father as one of their physical ancestors. Belief that Jesus had children is essentially a denial of the Incarnation, and thus a denial of the very basis of the Christian Faith.

Error in the Church

The Church is a human institution. It is made up of human beings, none of whom is perfect. Although it is the Body of Christ on earth, it is still not the perfected, heavenly Body of Christ. That awaits us at the gates of heaven. Meanwhile, we are called to be the best we can. We are called to be holy. But the Church is not always holy, either collectively or individually. Popes are imperfect. Bishops are imperfect. Priests and deacons are imperfect. Laypeople are imperfect. Parish councils, denominational councils, and even the College of

---

sexual relations with Joseph or any other human being. Since evidence shows that Mary was very young when Jesus was born, her virginity in the technical sense is a good assumption, but not a necessary one for her to be the *Theotokos*, the "Bearer of God."

Cardinals is imperfect. History is so full of examples that it hardly warrants further discussion.

The Church has a tenuous relationship with modern knowledge. Galileo was an example. When he demonstrated that the earth went around the sun, and not the other way around, the Church didn't want to accept it. Although this knowledge became commonplace (it is after all a simple fact), it took the Church several centuries to formally admit its error.

Similar things are going on with human sexuality. There is a huge misunderstanding of sexuality in society, and therefore in the Church. When the Church condemned Galileo's thought, the average person thought the Church was right and agreed. Likewise with sexuality today.

If you asked the average person on the street if heterosexuality was natural, the vast majority would say "yes." People do not really think about what "heterosexuality" is – they think of sex between males and females, but in fact "heterosexuality" is the idea of limiting sexual behavior to *only* male-female interactions. Anyone who has ever had more than one dog of the same sex knows that this is definitely not natural. Mammals are simply sexual. "Heterosexuality" and "homosexuality" are human inventions. It is natural for male mammals and female mammals to mate. It is not natural for mammals to think that sexual actions should be limited to such specific reproductive interactions or that it is somehow "wrong" to act sexually toward another of the same sex.

So the Church continues to teach things that are contrary to nature and furthermore asserts that these teachings somehow reflect "natural law." Think about Galileo. Nature stands by itself, waiting to be explored and understood by us. But it is not defined by us. The earth and sun didn't switch positions when Galileo observed them. They didn't switch positions when the Church officially accepted the solar system's heliocentricity. They remained where they had been for over four billion years. Likewise, all four of my dogs, two males and two females, will continue to express a variety of sexual activities with one another, even though three of the four are neutered.

In spite of being aware of its errors regarding the solar system's design, the Vatican continues to be one of the most backward and narrow-minded organizations with regard to human sexuality. Just as it tried to discredit the science of 17th century astronomy, so it ignores the science of 21st century psychology.

The *Catechism* (§2357) states that "Tradition has always declared that 'homosexual acts are intrinsically disordered.' They are contrary to the natural law."

The American Psychiatric Association (the national association of psychiatrists, medical doctors specializing in mental disorders) adopted an official position in 1992 that states, "Whereas homosexuality per se implies no impairment in judgment, stability, reliability, or general social or vocational capabilities, the American Psychiatric Association (APA) calls on all international health organizations, psychiatric organizations, and individual psychiatrists in other countries to urge the repeal in their own countries of legislation that penalizes homosexual acts by consenting adults in private. Further, APA calls on these organizations and individuals to do all that is possible to decrease the stigma related to homosexuality wherever and whenever it may occur."[77]

The American Psychological Association (the national association of psychologists) discusses whether homosexuality is a disorder on its website, "lesbian, gay, and bisexual orientations are not disorders. Research has found no inherent association between any of these sexual orientations and psychopathology. Both heterosexual behavior and homosexual behavior are normal aspects of human sexuality. Both have been documented in many different cultures and historical eras. Despite the persistence of stereotypes that portray lesbian, gay, and bisexual people as disturbed, several decades of research and clinical experience have led all mainstream medical and mental health organizations in this country to conclude that these orientations represent normal forms of human experience. Lesbian, gay, and bisexual relationships are normal forms of human bonding. Therefore, these mainstream organizations long ago abandoned classifications of homosexuality as a mental disorder."[78]

Thus today the Vatican is in exactly the same place with respect to science that it was in 1633 when Galileo Galilei was found "'vehemently suspect of heresy,' namely of having held the opinions that the sun lies motionless at the centre of the universe, that the earth is not at its center and moves, and that one may hold and defend an opinion as probable after it has been

---

[77] See the APA website, http://www.psych.org/Departments/EDU/Library/APAOfficialDocumentsandRelated/Position-Statement-on-Homosexuality.aspx
[78] See the website http://www.apa.org/helpcenter/sexual-orientation.aspx

declared contrary to Holy Scripture. He was required to 'abjure, curse and detest' those opinions."[79]

In spite of the Vatican's views of "nature" and "natural law," the earth continues to revolve around the sun as the sun itself revolves around the galactic center, and Tuggy and Wolfy (my two male dogs) occasionally show sexual interest in one another, just as Kansas and Maxine (my two female dogs) also occasionally show sexual interest in one another. Simply put, the Church, even in official teachings, can and does err on matters of scientific knowledge. Nature is an abundant, exuberant diversity – ours to explore, not to constrain.

Perhaps we are best returning to the *Sancta Mater Ecclesia* issue and using it to our advantage. We are all familiar with imperfect human parents because all of us had them. Some were worse than others, and some were downright evil, though for the most part parents try to do the best for their children.

One of the classic examples of how the Ten Commandments can contradict themselves is "What do I do if my mother tells me to kill my neighbor?" If all the commandments are equal and morality is simply black and white, then this is a true dilemma since one commandment says "Honor your father and mother" and another says "You shall not kill." If you kill your neighbor, you break the commandment against murder. If you don't kill your neighbor, you have not honored your mother's wish.

Few people would see this as a real dilemma. Those of us looking upon it as an example simply picture an evil and deranged murderous woman trying to get her child to assist her in her evil ways. The answer seems obvious, "You don't have to obey a parent when the parent is wrong."

For the child raised by this mother, however, the situation may be much less clear. Perhaps the mother has taught her children that the first and most important commandment is "Honor your mother and father." She would not be the first person to use the Bible selectively to achieve her own personal twisted goals. Perhaps she is even a serial killer and has never taught her children that murder was wrong. She had some rationalization when her children asked her about reading "You shall not kill" in a Bible they came across at a friend's

---

[79] See, for example, Eman McMullin, ed. *The Church and Galileo.* 2005, Notre Dame, IN: University of Notre Dame Press.

house. Perhaps this child never really thinks twice about the moral dilemma and thinks it is OK to kill the neighbor; after all, that's what Mama wants.

Yet that does not make it right. We have to back out of the emotional situation, the situation of parental manipulation, control, and misinformation, and grasp the larger picture. Our mother is not always right.

Thus with the Church. "Holy Mother Church" is not always right. "She" was wrong with Galileo and not only impeded science, but started the ignorant polarization of science and religion that still plagues us today, leaving some people mired in false beliefs like the denial of evolution and others with the false concept that religion is inherently backward and unnecessary. Both science and religion lose in that scenario, and humanity is starved in the process.

Today "Mother" is wrong when it comes to sexuality. "She" preaches against birth control in a world with exponential overpopulation. "She" preaches against divorce, even when the marriage is bad for both partners. "She" obsesses with the lie that the existence of same-sex marriage somehow denigrates the value of different-sex marriage. "She" calls homosexual acts "intrinsically disordered"[80] when in fact "several decades of research and clinical experience have led all mainstream medical and mental health organizations in this country to conclude that these orientations represent normal forms of human experience."

The man who spoke the truth about the earth and the sun was declared "vehemently suspect of heresy" for speaking the truth.

"Mother" was wrong once and "she" is wrong again.

We did not lose faith because the Church was wrong about Galileo. By some miracle (which I don't understand given their ridiculous views about evolution) even die-hard fundamentalists accept the solar system's heliocentricity. In spite of its error with Galileo, the Church continued to be the Body of Christ (though imperfect), continued to bring the Gospel of Salvation to the world, continued to celebrate the Sacred Mysteries, and continued to worship and adore God.

---

[80] *Catechism of the Catholic Church*, ¶2357, which in turn cites the Congregation for the Doctrine of the Faith, *Persona humana 8*.

The Church continues to do all that now, in spite of its errors on sexuality. We must not abandon faith, worship, and communion just because the Church is wrong on sexual issues. We must see this in the same light as Galileo, understanding that the Church can and does make technical errors, standing up to it, correcting it, even ignoring it on these issues, but still knowing that it is the Body of Christ. We must have hope and faith that, just as it has finally done with Galileo, the Church will eventually correct itself with regard to birth control, sexuality, and marriage equality. Many of the Protestant denominations are leading the way, and it is only a matter of time when the entire Church will be there.

Let's pray it takes less than 300 years this time around.

Salvation, Scripture, and Sexuality
5th Edition

ISBN 978-1-881568-23-0   **15.00**

ISBN 1-881568-23-7

9 781881 568230   90000

Healing Spirit Press

8539 Barnwood Lane ✠ Riverside, CA 92508 ✠ (951) 780-9932
HealingSpirit@ecchurch.org
www.ecchurch.org/healingspirit.htm

* 9 7 8 1 8 8 1 5 6 8 2 3 0 *